I0114211

SUSTAINABILITY

AND ITS

APPLICATIONS

Matthew N. O. Sadiku
&
Paul A. Adekunte

Copyright © 2024 Matthew N. O. Sadiku & Paul A. Adekunte

All rights reserved. No part of this publication may be reproduced, distributed, or transmitted in any form or by any means, including photocopying, recording, or other electronic or mechanical methods, without the prior written permission of the publisher, except as permitted by U.S. copyright law. For permission requests, contact:

support@bookfilmsmedia.com

Date published: 2024

Matthew N. O. Sadiku
 sadiku@ieee.org
 www.matthew-sadiku.com

Paul A. Adekunte
 adekuntepaul@gmail.com

Paperback: *979-8-9905496-9-2*
eBook: *979-8-9908049-0-6*
Hardcover: *979-8-9915027-2-6*

BookFilmsMedia
 2780 South Jones Blvd Suite 200- 4007
 Las Vegas, NV 89146 United States
 +1 725-238-6534

DEDICATED TO OUR WIVES:

JANET O. SADIKU

&

COMFORT A. ADEKUNTE

CONTENTS

PREFACE

Almost everything man does on earth has implications for the environment, economy, or society. Our world and the future we want are at risk. The development of humanity over the last decades has led to the increasingly unfavorable climate changes, natural disasters, wars, population explosion, poverty, ignorance and disease, gender inequality, the pollution of our surroundings, the stockpiling of nuclear weapons, and political and socio-economic instability. Responsible behavior that will ensure the long-term exploitation of resources without jeopardizing future generations aligns with the concept of sustainability. The notion of sustainability rose to prominence when the modern environmental activists rebuked the unsustainable character of contemporary societies where patterns of resource use, growth, and consumption threatened the integrity of ecosystems and the well-being of future generations

Sustainability is one of the most pressing challenges of our time across a wide spectrum of social, environmental, and economic matters. It is the quality of not being harmful to the environment or depleting natural resources. It creates and maintains the conditions under which humans and nature can exist in productive harmony, that permit fulfilling the social, economic, and other requirements of present and future generations. Sustainability, in one form or another, has been a concern for economists for well over 200 years. Global warming is the main reason for sustainability implementation. Major issues such as climate change, economic inequality, poverty, and social injustice are affecting people throughout the world. Sustainability is a broad topic that applies to a wide range of fields. It simply means the ability to maintain or support a process continuously over time. It is meeting the needs of the present without compromising the ability of future generations to meet their own needs. It is all about doing good for the environment and society at large.

This book explores the concept of sustainability and its various applications. It is organized into nine chapters that summarize sustainability and its applications.

Chapter 1: Introduction:

This chapter is designed to introduce the reader to the concept of sustainability. It serves as an introduction to the entire book. Sustainability is a measure of something's ability to continue. Sustainability is at the core of concepts such as sustainable cities, sustainable business, sustainable engineering, sustainable healthcare, sustainable manufacturing, sustainable agriculture, etc. It covers some of these popular applications.

Chapter 2: Sustainable Development:

In this chapter, we introduce the reader to sustainable development, its importance, and application areas. It discusses the 17 Sustainable Development Goals (SDGs), adopted by the United Nations. Sustainable development refers to the development that meets the present needs without compromising the ability of future generations to meet their own needs. It describes the holistic, systems-based approach that ensures sustainability. In economic terms, sustainable development is the "development that lasts."

Chapter 3: Sustainable Cities:

This chapter addresses what sustainable cities are all about. It specifies how to create sustainable cities and provides examples of sustainable cities. The majority of the world is now urban and the world is becoming increasingly urbanized. A sustainable city is a city designed with consideration for the triple bottom line: social, economic, environmental impact. To be truly sustainable, a city must be sustainable in all areas.

Chapter 4: Sustainable Engineering:

This chapter provides an introduction to the field of sustainable engineering. Engineering is the application of scientific and mathematical principles for practical purposes such as the design and operation of products and processes. Sustainable engineering may be regarded as engineering for human development that meets the needs of the present without compromising the ability of future generations to meet their own needs. It is the process of using resources in a way that is environmentally friendly. Sustainable engineers work to design systems and products that minimize pollution and conserve resources.

Chapter 5: Sustainable Business:

The chapter discusses what sustainable business is all about. Businesses use huge amounts of our planet's resources, and they in turn have huge impacts. Sustainability in business refers to a company's strategy and actions to eliminate the adverse environmental and social impacts caused by business operations. A sustainable business is one that ensures no harm to the environment and society. It implies balancing social, economic, and environmental considerations in business decision-making while maintaining a profit.

Chapter 6: Sustainable Healthcare:

In this chapter, we summarizes the healthcare sector's environmental footprint and the potential for reducing that footprint by applying the principles and tools of sustainability science. Healthcare systems can be regarded as all the activities whose primary purpose is to promote, restore, and maintain health. But healthcare is a significant contributor to climate change and environmental degradation. Sustainable health is a personal commitment to maintaining and taking responsibility for your own health, through preventative means. Sustainable healthcare may regarded as healthcare services of better quality, more affordable, with less impact on the planet, and that can be accessed by people equally and efficiently.

Chapter 7: Sustainable Manufacturing:

This chapter describes sustainable manufacturing and how environmental sustainability helps in achieving it. Manufacturers are under pressure by regulations and consumers to reduce the environmental impact of their activities. Today, humans are consuming natural resources through manufacturing activities at an alarming rate, which is not sustainable. Sustainable manufacturing is manufacturing products through economically-sound processes that minimize negative environmental impacts while conserving energy and natural resources. The goal of sustainable manufacturing is to minimize waste, maximize resource efficiency, and reduce the environmental impact of manufacturing.

Chapter 8: Sustainable Agriculture:

This chapter explains sustainable agriculture and some factors affecting it. Agriculture is one of the biggest threats to a healthy environment. Meeting the rapidly increasing global food demand with existing farming agricultural practices is likely going to lead to more intense competition for natural resources and land degradation. Sustainable agriculture is one that produces abundant food while protecting the environment and maintaining soil fertility. It refers to farming that is good for the environment, animals, and people.

Chapter 9: Sustainable Energy:

This chapter reviews major types of sustainable energy and their usage. Energy is the capacity to do work. Energy resources help in creating wealth and improving living standards. Sustainable energy is a significant aspect of sustainability. It is energy that is capable of meeting the energy needs of the present without compromising the resources and energy supply of the future. It is a form of energy that can be utilized again and again without putting a source in danger of getting depleted. It is generated from sources such as solar, wind, geothermal, and biomass.

This book is designed to introduce the reader to the concept of sustainability. It is a comprehensive introductory text on the issues, ideas, theories, principles, practices, and problems on sustainability. It provides an overview on each of its applications so that beginners can understand sustainability and its increasing importance and relevance. Everything is written in an easy-to-understand language. It is a must-read book for anyone who wants to learn about the sustainability, which is undoubtedly one of the major global issues in the 21th century. For anyone with influence on energy policy, whether in government, business or a campaign group, this book should be compulsory reading.

I am grateful to Ann Sadiku for drawing some of the figures. Special thanks are due our wives Dr. Janet Sadiku and Comfort Adekunte for helping in various ways.

— M. N. O. Sadiku

ABOUT THE AUTHOR

Matthew N. O. Sadiku:

He received his B. Sc. degree in 1978 from Ahmadu Bello University, Zaria, Nigeria and his M.Sc. and Ph.D. degrees from Tennessee Technological University, Cookeville, TN in 1982 and 1984 respectively. In total, he received seven college degrees. From 1984 to 1988, he was an assistant professor at Florida Atlantic University, Boca Raton, FL, where he did graduate work in computer science. From 1988 to 2000, he was at Temple University, Philadelphia, PA, where he became a full professor. From 2000 to 2002, he was with Lucent/Avaya, Holmdel, NJ as a system engineer and with Boeing Satellite Systems, Los Angeles, CA as a senior scientist. He is presently a Regents professor emeritus of electrical and computer engineering at Prairie View A&M University, Prairie View, TX.

He is the author of over 1,150 professional papers and over 120 books including "Elements of Electromagnetics" (Oxford University Press, 7th ed., 2018), "Fundamentals of Electric Circuits" (McGraw-Hill, 7th ed.,2020, with C. Alexander), "Computational Electromagnetics with MATLAB" (CRC Press, 4th ed., 2019), "Principles of Modern Communication Systems" (Cambridge University Press, 2017, with S. O. Agbo), and "Emerging Internet-based Technologies" (CRC Press, 2019). In addition to the engineering books, he has written Christian books including "Secrets of Successful Marriages," "How to Discover God's Will for YourLife," and commentaries on all the books of the New Testament Bible. Some of his books have been translated into French, Korean, Chinese (and Chinese Long Form in Taiwan), Italian, Portuguese, Spanish, German, Dutch, Polish, and Russian.

He was the recipient of the 2000 McGraw-Hill/Jacob Millman Award for outstanding contributions in the field of electrical engineering. He was also the recipient of Regents Professor award for 2012-2013 by the Texas A&M University System. He is a registered professional engineer and a life fellow of the Institute of Electrical and Electronics Engineers (IEEE) "for contributions to computational electromagnetics and engineering education." He was the IEEE Region 2 Student Activities Committee Chairman. He was an associate editor for IEEE Transactions on Education. He is also a member of Association for Computing Machinery (ACM) and American Society of Engineering Education (ASEE). His current research interests are in the areas of computational electromagnetic, computer science/ networks, engineering education, and marriage counseling. His works can be found in his autobiography, "My Life and Work" (Trafford Publishing, 2017) or his website: www. matthew-sadiku.com. He currently resides with his wife Janet in Westlake Florida. He can be reached via email at sadiku@ieee.org.

Paul A. Adekunte:

He received his B.Sc in zoology from Ahmadu Bello University, Zaria, Nigeria in 1983 and masters degree in crime management and prevention from Bayero University, Kano, Nigeria in 2011. He got his postgraduate degree in Biology in 2005 from the Federal College of Education (Technical) Akoka, Lagos, Nigeria. He also obtained certificates in public relations and computer studies. He is a professional educator in biology at the secondary and advanced levels as well a security expert. He is a member of several professional bodies.

His current areas of research interests include management, educational guidance and counseling, conflict and crisis resolution, and security matters. He has published several professional papers. He currently resides with his wife in Lagos, Nigeria and can be reached via email at adekuntepaul@gmail.com.

TABLE OF CONTENTS

CHAPTER 1
INTRODUCTION

"The first rule of sustainability is to align with natural forces, or at least try not to defy them."

– Hawken

1.1 INTRODUCTION

Since the creation of the United Nations (UN), the world's peoples have aspired to make progress on the great global issues of peace, security, freedom, development, and environment. These global issues remain prominent aspirations, and it has long been acknowledged that they are closely interlinked. Sustainability is one of the most pressing challenges of our time across a wide spectrum of social, environmental and economic matters. Major issues such as climate change, economic inequality, and social injustice are affecting people throughout the world. We all depend on Earth's natural resources, and taking care of them should be our priority.

Our world has finite resources. Our societal focus on endless growth and consumption is rapidly depleting these resources. Current business practices negatively impact our forests and oceans. Today a company must work to safeguard the health and security of their employees. The company's strategy and planning must include opportunities and risks related to climate change and a lower-emission future [1]. It must stay competitive in a rapidly changing landscape by implementing integrated sustainability strategies.

Sustainability is one of the most pressing challenges of our time across a wide spectrum of social, environmental, and economic matters. It is the quality of not being harmful to the environment or depleting natural resources. Global warming is the main reason for sustainability implementation. Major issues such as climate change, economic inequality, poverty, and social injustice are affecting people throughout the world. Sustainability is a broad topic that applies to a wide range of fields. It is meeting the needs of the present without compromising the ability of future generations to meet their own needs. The key principle of sustainable development underlying all others is the integration of environmental, social, and economic concerns into all aspects of decision making processes in order to move towards development that is truly sustainable [2].

This chapter is designed to introduce the reader to the concept of sustainability. It serves as an introduction to the entire book. It begins with explaining what sustainability is all about. It provides some applications of sustainability. It highlights the benefits and challenges of sustainability. The last section concludes with comments.

1.2 CONCEPT OF SUSTAINABILITY

Sustainability is often understood as a form of intergenerational ethics in which the environmental and economic actions taken by present generation do not diminish the opportunities of future generation to enjoy similar levels of wealth, utility, or welfare. The notion of sustainability rose to prominence when the modern environmental activists rebuked the unsustainable character of contemporary societies where patterns of resource use, growth, and consumption threatened the integrity of ecosystems and the well-being of future generations.

Sustainability, in one form or another, has been a concern for economists for well over 200 years. The concept of sustainability was originally coined in forestry, where it means never harvesting more than what the forest yields in new growth. The term "sustainability" has become popular in policy-oriented research as an expression of what public policies ought to achieve. The principal inspiration came from the Brundtland Report of 1987. Since then the concept has shifted in meaning [3].

The "Three Pillars of Sustainability" describes what sustainable development is all about. This tool conveys that sustainability consists of environmental, social, and economic factors that are vital when discussing the topic. The pillars are illustrated in Figure 1.1 and explained as follows [4,5]:

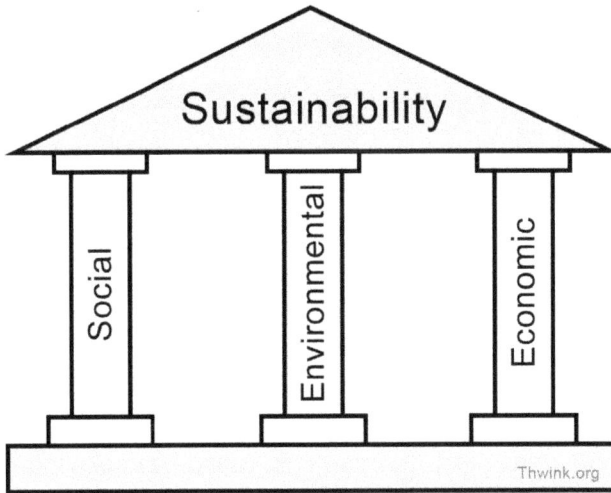

Figure 1.1 The three pillars of sustainability [4].

• *Environmental Sustainability* symbolizes the importance of things like natural resources and biodiversity to support life on Earth. This seems to be the most obvious pillar. Environmental sustainability occurs when humanity's rate of consumption does not exceed nature's rate of replenishment and when humanity's rate of generating pollution and emitting greenhouse gases does not exceed nature's rate of restoration. It relies on governmental initiatives to orient production and consumption into less environmentally destructive channels. Managing long-term environmental issues such as climate change and the loss of biodiversity is of critical importance to efforts to achieve sustainability. What is conducive to environmental sustainability remains a matter of debate.

• *Social Sustainability* places importance on social structures, well-being, and harmony; all factors that poverty, wars, and injustices can affect. This is the ability of a society to uphold universal human rights and meet people's basic needs, such as healthcare, education, and transportation.

• *Economic Sustainability* describes the ability of an economy to grow. Economics is the study of the allocation of limited resources across unlimited wants. We cannot have it all because there is not enough land, labor or capital (economic resources) to do so. Thus, we must decide what resources are best used to produce what goods [6]. Economic sustainability is the ability of human communities around the world to maintain their independence and have access to the resources required to meet their needs, meaning that secure sources of livelihood are available to everyone. This is especially important in today's societies, at a time when many sustainable initiatives require financing and a strong economic rationale.

In addition to these three pillars, we also have three pillars of sustainability with physical electronics as in Figure 1.2 [7]. Numerous practices are cited as threats to sustainability, such as political corruption, social inequality, the arms race, and profligate government expenditures.

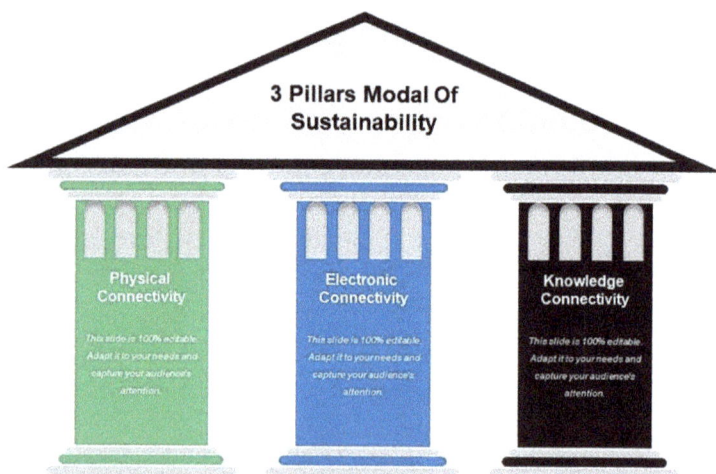

Figure 1.2 The three pillars of sustainability with physical electronics [7].

Organizations must act now to position themselves effectively within these ecosystems and maximizing their share of the opportunity ahead of competitors and other ecosystem players, shown in Figure 1.3 [8].

Figure 1.3 Players in sustainability ecosystems [8].

1.3 APPLICATIONS OF SUSTAINABILITY

Sustainability is a measure of something's ability to continue. Sustainability is at the core of concepts such as sustainable society, sustainable cities, sustainable development, sustainable energy, sustainable business, sustainable engineering, sustainable healthcare, sustainable manufacturing, sustainable infrastructure, and sustainable agriculture. We will consider some of these here [9]:

•   *Sustainable Development:* In contemporary debate, the term "sustainability" often serves as a synonym for "sustainable development," which refers to the social-ecological process to achieve sustainability. Sustainable development may also be regarded as a process of social advancement that accommodates the needs of current and future generations and that successfully integrates economic, social, and environmental considerations in decision making. In 2015, the 2030 Agenda for Sustainable Development was adopted by the UN. It provides a global framework for national strategies and policies to put the world on a path to sustainability. One of the most important elements of this were the 17 Sustainable Development Goals (SDGs) which set out various goals that the international community must work together to achieve. These goals are displayed in Figure 1.4 [4].

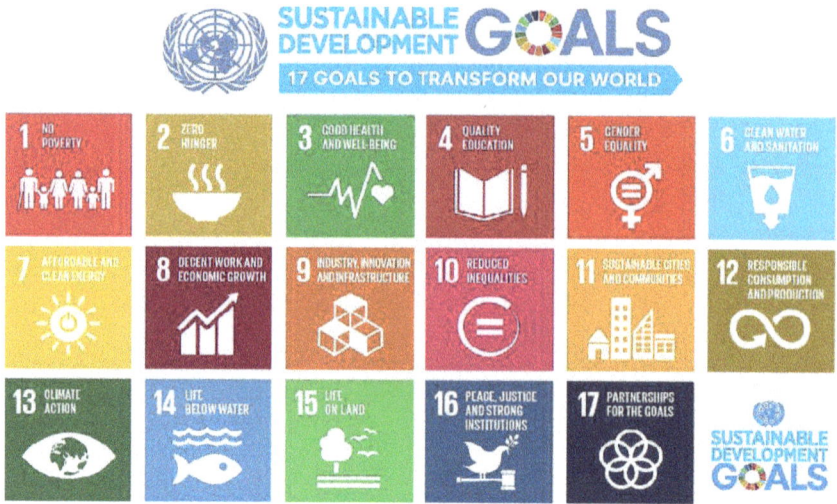

Figure 1.4 The Sustainable Development Goals [4].

These ambitious goals entered into force on 1 January 2016. They provide key benchmarks for us to understand how sustainability is being achieved worldwide. It is needless to say that the goals are interrelated and they cannot be addressed in isolation. Although not all of the SDGs are met globally, significant progress has been made. People are becoming more aware of them and organizing around them. The SDGs cannot and should not be taken as universal due to conceptual and moral differences among different communities and peoples.

• *Sustainable Society:* Changing values and norms reflect the changing influences on the society. Sustainable society is a society that has learned to live within the boundaries established by ecological limits. It can be maintained as a collective and ongoing entity because practices that imposed excessive burdens upon the environment have been reformed or abolished. Poverty is a major societal problem and it is said to exist when people lack the means to satisfy their basic needs. In industrialized societies, the chief cause of poverty is fluctuations in the business cycle, with mass unemployment during periods of depression or serious recession. In many developing countries, the population grows even faster than the economy does and growth in the population out paces that of food, with no net reduction in poverty as a result. Thus an increase of the GNP does not necessarily lead to an improved standard of living for the citizens.

•   *Sustainable Healthcare:* When addressing sustainability, health practices also need to be addressed, as they affect sociality and relationality with the human and nonhuman dimensions of life. The health practices engage in practices of care, responsibility, and respect for the environment, land, and territory. Ethnomedicine is a field of study that has long investigated how indigenous peoples have made use of herbs, plants, and animal parts for curative and healing purposes. These long-standing health practices have gone hand in hand with the so-called 'Western' medical practices. The traditional healing measures have sometimes been incorporated into mainstream medicine [10]. The five dimensions of the 2030 Agenda—Prosperity, People, Planet, Peace, and Partnerships (The 5 P's)—articulate the scope of this vision and are depicted in Figure 1.5 [11].

Figure 1.5 The five dimensions of the 2030 Agenda [11].

•   *Sustainable Energy:* Ecologists have tended to approach sustainability in terms of physical interdependencies, energy flows, and population dynamics. We continue to rely upon fossil fuel energy, such as coal, oil, and gas, despite the negative impact on global temperature and air quality. Potentially renewable resources should be managed to conserve their long-term viability. Nonrenewable resources should be extracted at rates that allow an ordered transition to alternatives.

• Sustainable Business: Past business models focused on creating value for the business owner. These business models are incomplete because they do not calculate the effect a business has on the world, or the impact of those effects on the business itself. Continuing to rely on unsustainable business practices carries inherent risk. A sustainable business is one that takes a holistic approach. No business operates in isolation; it exists within an ecosystem. To continue generating value from the environment, an organization must calculate its effects on that environment. Sustainable business models can therefore be conceptualized as complete or holistic business models. A company must include the full impact of business practices on external stakeholders to determine the net value it produces. Sustainable practices are specific things a business does to increase sustainability. Typical examples involve reducing, reusing, and recycling materials or products. For example, a company may stop using paper altogether by switching to digital communications. Society is pressuring business leaders to generate value for the environmental. Long-term financial gain is only possible through sustainable development. Both start-ups and established businesses need to embrace sustainable business model within the fabric of their organization. This is the only way to ensure long term survival. Sustainable business models are illustrated in Figure 1.6 [12].

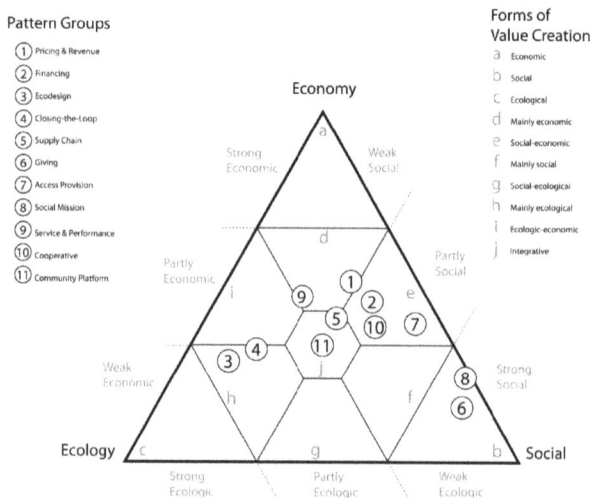

Figure 1.6 Sustainable business models [12].

1.4 BENEFITS

The benefits of green technology are of three types: environmental, economic, and social. Sustainability is all about doing good for the environment and society at large. Embedding sustainability in company's day-to-day operations can bring many direct benefits not only to society and economy, but to business itself. Sustainability can serve as a standard against which existing institutions are to be judged and as an objective toward which society should move. People are becoming more critical of corporate impacts on the global environment. Adopting an sustainable business model helps to create a positive brand image. Although there are some initial costs involved, these will soon be recuperated. Other benefits of sustainability include the following [13-15].

1.   *Reduces Energy Consumption:* Sustainability helps to reduce energy consumption by pursuing energy efficiency in every aspect of the product lifecycle. Sustainable product design will be applied to minimize the energy consumption of the finished product, enabling savings for both the business and the consumer. Sustainability is also helping to reduce the use of traditional non-renewable energy sources such as fossil fuels.

2.   *Reduces Energy Costs:* Waste disposal, water and energy consumption, and material use cost money. This cuts into profit. As you continue to do good for the environment, your energy costs will go down and this does good for both society and our planet at large.

3.   *Reduces Waste:* Sustainability is presented as an alternative to short-term, myopic, and wasteful behaviors. It is all about keeping the planet healthy and clean. This means using less energy, water, and other resources to cut down on expenses. You will also save money by utilizing recycled materials. Recycling has the benefit of turning waste into a resource.

4.   *Reduces Water Consumption:* Water is a precious resource on our planet and making sure it is not wasted is paramount. Sustainability helps to reduce water consumption. This can be achieved by using

green tech to improve the product design or to add smart functionality, allowing to save water by using only what is strictly necessary for the task.

5. *Improves Product Design and Performance:* The increased public awareness about sustainability has led to greater attention towards efficient and sustainable designs. Modern product design is leveraging powerful digital transformation technologies such as digital twins and machine learning to optimize product performance, longevity, manufacturing process, and lifecycle.

6. *Reduces Air Pollution:* Traffic and polluting industries are the major contributors to air pollution in our cities. Green technologies such as hybrid and electric vehicles are increasingly been used and incentivized to reduce air pollution in the cities and contribute to improving the standards of living. A green methodology that helps reduce air pollution in the cities is sustainable urban design, which makes it possible to increase the green areas with oxygen producing trees and improve ventilation.

7. *Reduces Carbon Footprint:* Reducing the carbon footprint is especially challenging for energy-intensive industries like mining. From green energy to recycling and more rational use of natural resources, green energy is going to play a big role in helping us reduce our carbon footprint.

8. *Builds Reputation:* Sustainability reporting makes it easier for a business owner to prove their worth to investors and build their reputation. Less time will be wasted on paperwork and finance rates may be lowered. These things influence the reputation and growth of a business.

9. *Reduces Risks:* A business owner may be able to catch issues before they cause a major problem. Legal proceedings and huge expenses could be prevented with sustainability reporting. Sustainable business practices lower costs, create more competitive advantages, foster opportunities for growth, reduce risks, and create the potential for more profit.

10. *Tax Incentives:* Governments are now supporting the journey towards sustainable development. Subsidies and tax incentives to

switch to green technologies are now very common in the United States and Europe. An additional advantage of green technology is being able to benefit from tax incentives and other grants that governments are supporting to promote the green revolution and help save the planet.

11.   *Risks Being Left Behind:* Sustainability is a major concern with today's business leaders. Business owners must embrace a sustainable brand image, or risk being left behind.

12.   *Increase Customer Trust:* Curating a sustainable brand image is a great way for businesses to build customer trust. This is because having a sustainable brand image makes your company appear to be more caring and thoughtful about its impact on the environment.

Some of these benefits are illustrated in Figure 1.7 [16].

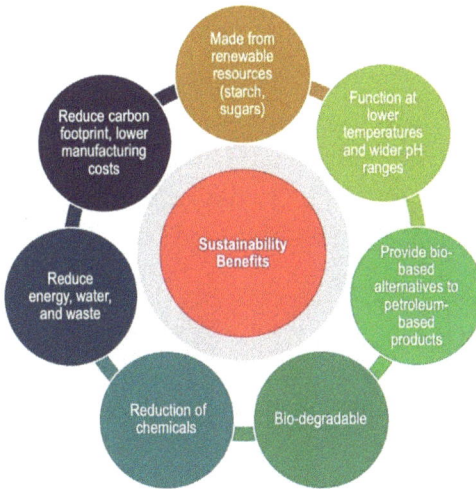

Figure 1.7 Some benefits of sustainability [16].

1.5 CHALLENGES

Sustainable development is an issue which should be treated very seriously as it affects everyone. There is contradiction between our desire for a better life and our concern for what this may do to the environment. Controversy over the substitutability of natural and human-made capital has divided proponents of weak and strong sustainability. For some environmentalists, true sustainability is possible only in small-scale communities, where humans can live in close contact with natural processes. While other radical environmentalists accept a high-tech postindustrial civilization; for them too there must be a clear break with existing economic practices and power structures.

Many economists believe we can maintain current consumption and that technological innovation will take care of the needs of future generations. However, other economists believe that created capital and natural capital are complementary goods; as we consume more created capital, we will also have to consume more natural capital. We understand that we cannot have our cake and eat it too. Other challenges of sustainability include the following [17,18].

1.   *Pollution:* Environmental problems are related to soil, water, air, etc. that are really important for the development of humans and the planet. Pollution (air and water) is a major hurdle in the way of sustainability. Plastic, motor vehicle exhaust, heavy metals, and chemicals are some pollutants. Clean water is necessary for life, and we are polluting our natural drinking water reservoirs by mixing pollutants. It is a big problem because these wastes pollute our drinking water and pose major threats to humans and their health. The burning of fossil fuels is also creating pollution as they release greenhouse gases.

2.   *Food Shortages:* The world is witnessing food scarcity due to the variation in weather conditions and soil degradation. This is a crucial issue in the future in the face of our growing population. The area of arable land currently available is diminishing due to deforestation which limits the availability of local food for people inhabiting areas near to the forests. Since 1960, an estimated one-third of the world's arable land has been lost through erosion and other degradations.

3.   *Overpopulation:* Right now, overpopulation is one of the biggest concerns because it has reached unsustainable levels. It leads to the scarcity of resources and is currently the central issue in environmental problems.

4.   *Depletion of Natural Resources:* The depletion of resources such as oil, food, and water is one of the main environmental issues. It is accelerating the issues such as air pollution, overpopulation, and

industrialization. Different countries are experiencing severe energy crises, and it is because of the depletion of natural resources, including fossil fuels.

5. *Deforestation:* Due to the deforestation for food, cloth, and shelter, we are losing our natural protection and polluting the environment. Instead of growing more trees, we are cutting green spaces for farms and housing. Governments and individuals are taking the initiative to grow plants.

6. *Climate Change:* This is another significant environmental issue that is increasing day by day. It is occurring because of the increasing global warming, rising temperature, and burning of fossil fuels. The change in weather pattern shows many challenges for the climate. Climate changes such as global warming are the consequence of human activities in the form of greenhouse gas emissions. It is leading to the rising temperature of the earth and oceans. These factors affect humans and nature in the form of severe changes in weather patterns, floods, and droughts.

7. *Raising Livestock:* The manner in which livestock is raised and the frequency with which it is being consumed is a major concern. Currently, livestock accounts for around 30% of the world's surface which is fit for raising animals and meet the high demand for meat and dairy products.

8. *Natural Disasters:* Natural occurrences, such as earthquakes and tsunamis, can pose a threat to sustainability as they can shift the flow of water and destroy certain elements of infrastructure.

9. *Corruption:* One of the most glaringly obvious social inequalities in developing nations is the corruption rampant in the government. Corruption is an act of bribery. It refers to private wealth-seeking behavior of someone who represents the state and public authority. It is the misuse of public goods by public officials, for private gains. Due to bureaucracy and corruption in some nations, in order to pass certain development projects a stipend needs to be paid to ministers as well as service fees to the government which significantly slow down NGO processes.

10. *Gender Inequality:* This is another rampant social issue

rampant. In rural regions of some developing nation, women are often left responsible for cultivating land and raising livestock. Economic abuse is commonly used against women with men claiming the entirety of access to shared funds and belittling women by monitoring their basic spending habits. Achieving female empowerment is one of the challenges of sustainable development, as extreme poverty is not a sustainable status quo.

11. *Rubbish:* In some nations, rubbish is everywhere. Streets, rivers, fields, being eaten in the middle of the road by a hungry goat or sacred cow. People lack the common knowledge on the recycling of rubbish. It is common to dump it all in landfills and hoping for the best without investing in appropriate infrastructure to reduce the rubbish. Figure 1.8 is an example of rubbish on the street [17].

Figure 1.8 Rubbish on the street [17].

12. *Unemployment and Poverty:* Due to old-fashioned practices and economic culture, it is hard to create jobs for people. As a result, we are witnessing unemployment and poverty in both emerging and developing markets.

1.6 CONCLUSION

Sustainability can be loosely described as a state of affairs where the sum of natural and man-made resources remains at least constant for the foreseeable future. It is about how we work and make decisions. It is as much about the culture of an organization as it is about technical aspects. It is the only way to protect ecological health, the natural environment, and humans. True sustainability offers indisputable value, from cost savings and risk management to improved stakeholder relations and public credibility. The concept of sustainability must incorporate the idea of regeneration. If a resource is used, like a tree, or water, it must be allowed to regenerate in order to be sustainable. Sustainable practices are specific to an organization, and each company integrates its programs with the organizational objectives. Sustainability is a top priority for most business leaders.

If you want to expand your knowledge of sustainability across various organizations, industries and practices, you should consider completing online courses on sustainability. The courses will cover topics such as climate change, renewable energy, water, agriculture, waste, green building, socially responsible business, ecosystem valuation, microlending, environmental justice, etc. The courses will develop the skills, confidence, and network to lead change in your sector, organization, and sphere of influence to make significant contributions to society. It will provide you with great experience to work in different areas including business, consulting, environmental, governance, and energy sectors. For more information on sustainability, one should consult books in [19-48] and the following related journals:

- *Sustainability*

- *Sustainability Next Magazine*

- *Nature Sustainability*

REFERENCE

[1]   "ExxonMobil is committed to improving quality of life by meeting the needs of society,"

https://corporate.exxonmobil.com/-/media/global/files/sustainability-report/2022-executive-summary.pdf#:~:text=ExxonMobil%20is%20committed%20to%20creating%20sustainable%20solutions%20that,the%20environment%20and%20the%20communities%20where%20we%20operate.

[2]   M. N. O. Sadiku, P. A. Adekunte, and J. O. Sadiku, "Sustainability 101," International Research Journal of Modernization in Engineering Technology and Science, vol. 6, no. 1, January 2024, pp.1476-1481.

[3]   T. Kuhlman and J. Farrington, "What is sustainability?" Sustainability, vol. 2, 2010, pp. 3436-3448.

[4]   A. Browne, "Explainer: What is sustainability and why is it important?" October 2022,

https://earth.org/what-is-sustainability/

[5]   "What is sustainability?"

https://www.mcgill.ca/sustainability/files/sustainability/what-is-sustainability.pdf

[6]   S. R. Elliot, "Sustainability: An economic perspective," Resources, Conservation and Recycling, vol. 44, no. 3, June 2005, pp. 263-277.

[7]   B. Sood, "1. Enlightenment- When the wheels of life took the turn," May 2015,

https://bhushansood.com/enlightenment/astrology-a-science-of-enlightened-and-enlightenment/

[8]   S. Milanese et al., "Overcoming the challenges to sustainability," July 2022,

https://www.adlittle.com/en/insights/report/overcoming-challenges-sustainability#:~:text=Overcoming%20the%20challenges%20to%20 sustainability%201%20Sustainability%20strategy,...%208%20 Integr-ate%20sustainability%20indicators%2C%20reporting%20 %26%20 tools

[9]   J. Meadowcroft, "Sustainability," December 2023,

https://www.britannica.com/science/sustainability

[10]   P. K. Virtanen, L. Siragusa, and H. Guttorm, "Introduction: Toward more inclusive definitions of sustainability," Current Opinion in Environmental Sustainability, vol. 43, April 2020, pp. 77-82.

[11]   "Understand sustainable development,"

https://trailhead.salesforce.com/content/learn/modules/the-global-goals/learn-about-the-global-goals

[12]   "Sustainable business models,"

https://strive2thrive.earth/sustainable-business-models/

[13]   "7 Benefits of sustainability in business," November 2021

https://www.technologytimesnow.com/benefits-of-sustainability-in-business/

[14]   "Top 10 benefits of green technology," December 2023,

https://sustainability-success.com/benefits-of-green-technology/#:~:text=TOP%2010%20Benefits%20of%20Green%20 Technology%201%201.,8.%20Reduces%20overall%20carbon%20 footprint%20...%20More%20items

[15]   "5 Benefits of sustainable business practices,"

https://www.jadetrack.com/5-benefits-of-sustainable-business-practices/

[16]   "Sustainability & environment,"

https://www.enzymetechnicalassociation.org/enzymes/ sustainability-2/

[17]   "Sustainable development and its challenges in developing countries," August 2018,

https://medium.com/@iynf/sustainable-development-and-its-challenges-in-developing-countries-487a333184a0

[18] "Biggest challenges to achieve sustainable environmental issues," February 2022,

https://wiselancer.net/biggest-challenges-to-achieve-sustainable-natural-environmental/

[19]   M. N. O. Sadiku, Emerging Green Technologies. Boca Raton, FL: CRC Press, 2020.

[20]   N. Munier, Introduction to Sustainability. Amsterdam, The Netherlands: Springer, 2005.

[21]   G. C. Gallopín, A Systems Approach to Sustainability and Sustainable Development. ECLAC, 2003.

[22]   A. Espinosa and J. Walker, Complexity Approach to Sustainability, A: Theory and Application. World Scientific, 2017.

[23]   R. Dyball and B. Newell, Understanding Human Ecology: A Systems Approach to Sustainability. Routledge, 2014.

[24]   I. Christie and D. Warburton.From Here to Sustainability: Politics in The Real World. Routledge, 2010.

[25]   T. O'Riordan, The Transition to Sustainability: The Politics of Agenda 21 In Europe. Routledge, 2013. [26] S. S. Muthu (ed.), Sustainability in The Textile Industry. Singapore: Springer, 2017.

[27]   P. Murray, The Sustainable Self: A Personal Approach to Sustainability Education. Routledge, 2012.

[28]   B. Elzen, F. W. Geels, and K. Green (eds.), System Innovation and The Transition to Sustainability: Theory, Evidence and Policy. Edward Elgar Publishing, 2004.

[29]   S. Van den Bosch, Transition Experiments: Exploring Societal Changes Towards Sustainability. 2010.

[30]   M. Robertson, Sustainability Principles and Practice. Routledge, 2021.

[31]   D. Hitchcock and M. Willard, The Business Guide to

Sustainability: Practical Strategies and Tools For Organizations. Routledge, 2012.

[32]   A. Remmen, Life Cycle Management: A Business Guide to Sustainability. UNEP/Earthprint, 2007.

[33]   O. Langhelle, Towards Sustainable Development: On the Goals of Development-And the Conditions Of Sustainability. Springer, 1999.

[34]   G. Weybrecht, The Sustainable MBA: A Business Guide to Sustainability. John Wiley & Sons, 2013.

[35]   National Research Council, Our Common Journey: A Transition Toward Sustainability. National Academies Press, 1999.

[36]   M. Leach et al., Understanding Governance: Pathways to Sustainability. STEPS Centre, 2007.

[37]   M. Dove and D. Kammen, Science, Society and The Environment: Applying Anthropology and Physics to Sustainability. Routledge, 2015.

[38]   R. Brinkmann, Introduction to Sustainability. Wiley-Blackwell, 2nd edition, 2021.

[39]   K. A. Parker, Introduction: Sustainability in Higher Education. Routledge, 2012.

[40]   H. Atkinson and R. Wade (ed.), The challenge of sustainability: Linking politics, education and learning. Policy Press, 2014.

[41]   M. Mulligan, An Introduction to Sustainability: Environmental, Social and Personal Perspectives. New York: Routledge, 2014.

[42]   P. P. Rogers, K. F. Jalal, and J. A. Boyd. An Introduction to Sustainable Development. Earthscan, 2012.

[43]   J. Elliott, An Introduction to Sustainable Development. Routledge, 2012.

[44]   P. L. Schiller and J. Kenworthy, An Introduction to Sustainable Transportation: Policy, Planning and Implementation. Routledge, 2017.

[45]   T. P. Soubbotina, Beyond Economic Growth: An Introduction to Sustainable Development. World Bank Publications, 2004.

[46]   T. Pfister, M. Schweighofer, and A. Reichel, Sustainability. Routledge, 2016.

[47]   J. L. Caradonna, Sustainability: A History. Oxford University Press, 2022.

[48]   S. Schaltegger, R. Burritt, and H. Petersen, An Introduction to Corporate Environmental Management: Striving for Sustainability. Routledge, 2017.

CHAPTER 2
SUSTAINABLE DEVELOPMENT

"Sustainable development is the pathway to the future we want for all. It offers a framework to generate economic growth, achieve social justice, exercise environmental stewardship and strengthen governance."

– Ban Ki-moon

2.1 INTRODUCTION

Almost everything man does on earth has implications for the environment, economy, or society. Our world and the future we want are at risk. The development of humanity over the last decades has led to the increasingly unfavorable climate changes, natural disasters, wars, population explosion, poverty, ignorance and disease, gender inequality, the pollution of our surroundings, the stockpiling of nuclear weapons, and political and socio-economic instability. Responsible behavior that will ensure the long-term exploitation of resources without jeopardizing future generations aligns with the concept of sustainability. The term "sustainability" is often referred to as "sustainable development." Sustainability is regarded as a paradigm for thinking about balancing environmental, economic, and social needs for the present and future. Sustainable development describes the holistic, systems-based approach that ensures sustainability. The term is often used in business, government, and non-profit organizations to refer to the processes required to balance economic growth, environmental stewardship, and social inclusion.

Sustainability is the capacity to maintain some entity, outcome or process over time. Sustainable development (SD) refers to the development that meets the present needs without compromising the ability of future generations to meet their own needs. It means refining the problem caused by continuous economic growth. It is the development that meets the needs of the present without compromising the future. SD is the bridge between environmental, economic and social goals, between north and south, between Governments, civil society and business, between science and policy, and between policy and action. The ultimate objective of sustainable development is to achieve a balance among environmental, economic, and social sustainability, making these the three pillars on which SD relies on. The sustainable development goals (SDGs) recognize strategies that improve health and education, reduce inequality, erase hunger, and spur economic growth. They map out a global vision for a better world. They set out ambitious goals and targets for people, prosperity, planet, and peace. To advance the sustainable development agenda every national government must integrate the SDGs into national plans and deliver the breakthroughs that our world desperately needs [1].

This chapter introduces the reader to sustainable development, its importance, and application areas. It begins with explaining the concepts of sustainability and sustainable development. It discusses the 17 Sustainable Development Goals (SDGs), adopted by the United Nations. It addresses five critical areas of importance of the SDGs. It considers the implications or applications of SDGs. It highlights the benefits and challenges of SDGs. The last section concludes with comments.

2.2 CONCEPT OF SUSTAINABILITY

A lot of development is unsustainable. It has taken us to climate change. Environmental destruction, conflict, war, poverty, hunger, vast inequalities, and social instability. Unsustainable development occurs when current progress is at the expense of future generations. This includes unsystematic planning that causes environmental degradation, such as the use of fossil fuels, or farming methods that cause damage to animals and ecosystems [2]. Unsustainable development happens when people pursue immediate rewards without thinking about harms to other people or the planet. Decision-makers need to be constantly mindful of the relationships among the three interconnected pillars, namely the environment, economy, and society. They must ensure responsible human behavior and actions at the international, national, community and individual levels.

The concept of sustainability is based on classical economics. Sustainable development can be interpreted in economic terms as "development that lasts." Sustainability is a social goal for people to co-exist on Earth over a long time. It is often understood as a form of intergenerational ethics in which the environmental and economic actions taken by present generation do not diminish the opportunities of future generation to enjoy similar levels of wealth, utility, or welfare. The notion of sustainability rose to prominence when the modern environmental activists rebuked the unsustainable character of contemporary societies where patterns of resource use, growth, and consumption threatened the integrity of ecosystems and the well-being of future generations.

Sustainability, in one form or another, has been a concern for economists for well over 200 years. The concept of sustainability was originally coined in forestry, where it means never harvesting more than what the forest yields in new growth. The term "sustainability" has become popular in policy-oriented research as an expression of what public policies ought to achieve. The principal inspiration came from the Brundtland Report of 1987. Since then the concept has shifted in meaning [3].

The "Three Pillars of Sustainability" describes what sustainable development is all about. This tool conveys that sustainability consists of environmental, social, and economic factors that are vital when discussing the topic. The pillars (or dimensions) are explained as follows [4,5]:

•   *Environmental sustainability* symbolizes the importance of things like natural resources and biodiversity to support life on Earth. This seems to be the most obvious pillar. Environmental sustainability is about the natural environment and how it remains productive and resilient to support human life. It occurs when humanity's rate of consumption does not exceed nature's rate of replenishment and when humanity's rate of generating pollution and emitting greenhouse gases does not exceed nature's rate of restoration. It relies on governmental initiatives to orient production and consumption into less environmentally destructive channels. For example, the effects of climate change provide a convincing argument for the need for environmental sustainability. Environmentally-friendly infrastructure is needed for increased economic output and productivity.

• *Social sustainability* places importance on social structures, well-being, and harmony; all factors that poverty, wars, and injustices can affect. It encompasses notions of equity, empowerment, accessibility, participation, cultural identity, and institutional stability. This is the ability of a society to uphold universal human rights and meet people's basic needs, such as healthcare, education, and transportation. Social sustainability is not about ensuring that everyone's needs are met. Rather, it aims at providing enabling conditions for everyone to have the capacity to realize their needs.

• *Economic sustainability* implies a system of production that satisfies present consumption levels without compromising future needs. Economics is the study of the allocation of limited resources across unlimited wants. Economies consist of markets where transactions occur. We cannot have it all because there is not enough land, labor or capital (economic resources) to do so. Thus, we must decide what resources are best used to produce what goods [5]. Economic sustainability is the ability of human communities around the world to maintain their independence and have access to the resources required to meet their needs. This is especially important in today's societies, at a time when many sustainable initiatives require financing and a strong economic rationale.

Numerous practices are cited as threats to sustainability, such as political corruption, social inequality, the arms race, and profligate government expenditures. Like sustainability, the three main dimensions of sustainable development are economic growth, environmental protection, and social equality, as depicted in Figure 2.1 [7]. These policies are often described as green because they focus on limiting the impact of development on the environment.

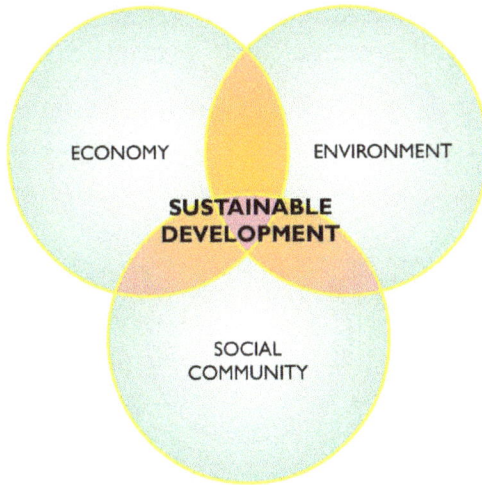

Figure 2.1 The three main dimensions of sustainable development [7]

2.3 WHAT IS SUSTAINABLE DEVELOPMENT?

In contemporary debate, the term "sustainability" often serves as a synonym for "sustainable development," which refers to the social-ecological process to achieve sustainability.

The concept of "sustainable development" is about steering humanity toward a sustainable future that does not deplete our natural resources. The desired result is a society where living conditions and resources meet human needs without undermining the planetary integrity and stability of the natural system. The term "sustainable development" gained wide popularity in the international community after the renowned report " Our Common Future" was published by the World Commission on Environment and Development in 1987. The idea of sustainable development grew from numerous environmental movements in earlier decades.

Sustainable development is the ability to make development sustainable to ensure that it meets the needs of the present without compromising the ability of future generations to meet their own needs. It may also be regarded as a process of social advancement that accommodates the needs of current and future generations and that successfully integrates economic, social, and environmental considerations in decision making. It is the mutually beneficial interaction between the legal interest of a business and the economy, government and politics, and civil society, and culture.

The three primary goals of sustainable development are [7]:

•　　To minimize the expenditure of natural resources while creating new developments.

•　　To create an environment that can be maintained and sustained without destroying the environment.

•　　To provide a method for rebuilding existing developments to make them eco-friendly facilities and projects.

International organizations such as NGOs, United Nations, aid organizations, and even governments are making continuous sponsoring efforts to ensure that the goal of sustainable development is achieved for every individual across the globe.

Some real-life examples of sustainable development include the following [8]:

•　　*Green spaces:* A perfect example of sustainable development manifestation is green spaces. Parks, lakes, and forests are essential to cooling cities. Trees produce oxygen and help filter out air pollution. Governments that design cities to prioritize green spaces often promote commuting by foot or bicycle, encouraging healthy lifestyles and well-being. Sustainable development focuses on eco-friendly building, green architecture, and other sustainable constructions.

•　　*Solar energy:* Renewable energy is a popular topic and it includes solar energy, hydropower, wind, and biomass fuels. Using the sun's energy to power electric grids can reduce emissions from power plants and other pollutants. You may have spotted solar panels on your rooftop. This technology continues to get cheaper and it is competitive with cost of electricity powered by fossil fuels. Hydro energy as used in turbines. Wind energy is often employed in windmills.

•　　*Sustainable finance:* is another widely impactful sustainable development practice. It covers a range of activities, from funding green energy projects to investing in companies that demonstrate strong social values. Sustainable development simply means that resources should be naturally used in such a way that they are not over-exploited.

Concepts like gender equality, poverty, ecological restoration, and natural resource conservation are all types of sustainable development.

2.4 SUSTAINABLE DEVELOPMENT GOALS

In 2015, the 2030 Agenda for Sustainable Development was adopted by the UN. It provides a global framework for national strategies and policies to put the world on a path to sustainability. One of the most important elements of this were the 17 Sustainable Development Goals (SDGs) which set out various goals that the international community must work together to achieve. These global goals aimed at improving the planet and the quality of human life around the world by the year 2030. In essence, the SDGs are a continuation of the eight Millennium Development Goals (MDGs), which began in the year 2000 and ended in 2015. The MDGs helped to lift nearly one billion people out of extreme poverty, combat hunger, and allow more girls to attend school. The 17 SDG goals address the global challenges, including poverty, inequality, climate change, environmental degradation, peace, and justice.

The SDG goals are displayed in Figure 2.2 [4].

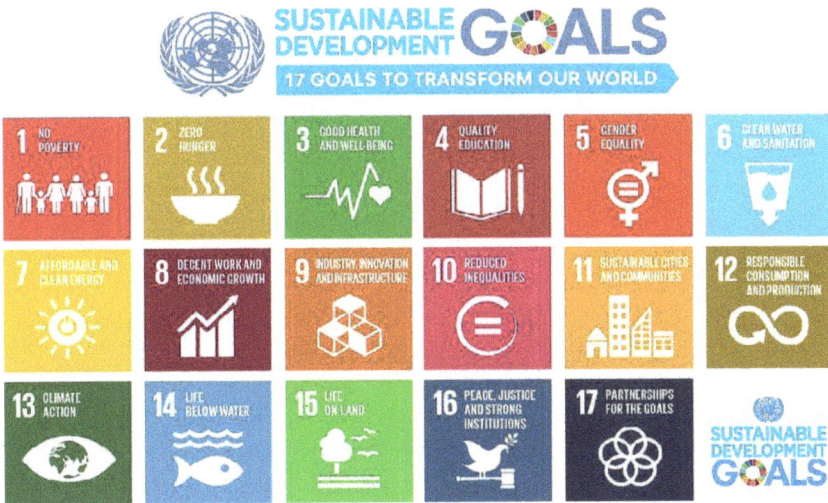

Figure 2. 2 The Sustainable Development Goals [4]

These ambitious goals entered into force on 1 January 2016. The

193 countries that make up the United Nations (UN) agreed to adopt the 2030 Agenda for Sustainable Development. The goals provide key benchmarks for us to understand how sustainability is being achieved worldwide. It is needless to say that the goals are interrelated and they cannot be addressed in isolation. Although not all of the SDGs are met globally, significant progress has been made. People are becoming more aware of them and organizing around them. The SDGs cannot and should not be taken as universal due to conceptual and moral differences among different communities and peoples.

In summary, the 17 goals are [9]:

- Goal 1: No Poverty: End poverty in all its forms everywhere.

- Goal 2: Zero Hunger: End hunger, achieve food security and improved nutrition and promote sustainable agriculture.

- Goal 3: Good Health and Well-being: Ensure healthy lives and promote well-being for all at all ages.

- Goal 4: Quality Education: Ensure inclusive and equitable quality education and promote lifelong learning opportunities for all.

- Goal 5: Gender Equality: Achieve gender equality and empower all women and girls.

- Goal 6: Clean Water and Sanitation: Ensure availability and sustainable management of water and sanitation for all.

- Goal 7: Affordable and Clean Energy: Ensure access to affordable, reliable, sustainable and modern energy for all.

- Goal 8: Decent Work and Economic Growth: Promote sustained, inclusive and sustainable economic growth, full and productive employment and decent work for all.

- Goal 9: Industry, Innovation, and Infrastructure: Build resilient infrastructure, promote inclusive and sustainable industrialization, and foster innovation.

- Goal 10: Reduced Inequality: Reduce inequality within and among countries.

• Goal 11: Sustainable Cities and Communities: Make cities and human settlements inclusive, safe, resilient, and sustainable.

• Goal 12: Responsible Consumption and Production: Ensure sustainable consumption and production patterns.

• Goal 13: Climate Action: Take urgent action to combat climate change and its impacts.

• Goal 14: Life Below Water: Conserve and sustainably use the oceans, seas, and marine resources for sustainable development.

• Goal 15: Life on Land: Protect, restore, and promote sustainable use of terrestrial ecosystems, sustainably manage forests, combat desertification, and halt and reverse land degradation and halt biodiversity loss.

• Goal 16: Peace, Justice, and Strong Institutions: Promote peaceful and inclusive societies for sustainable development, provide access to justice for all and build effective, accountable, and inclusive institutions at all levels.

• Goal 17: Partnerships to Achieve the Goal: Strengthen the means of implementation and revitalize the global partnership for sustainable development.

Key issues addressed by the 17 SDGs are summarized in Figure 2.3 [10].

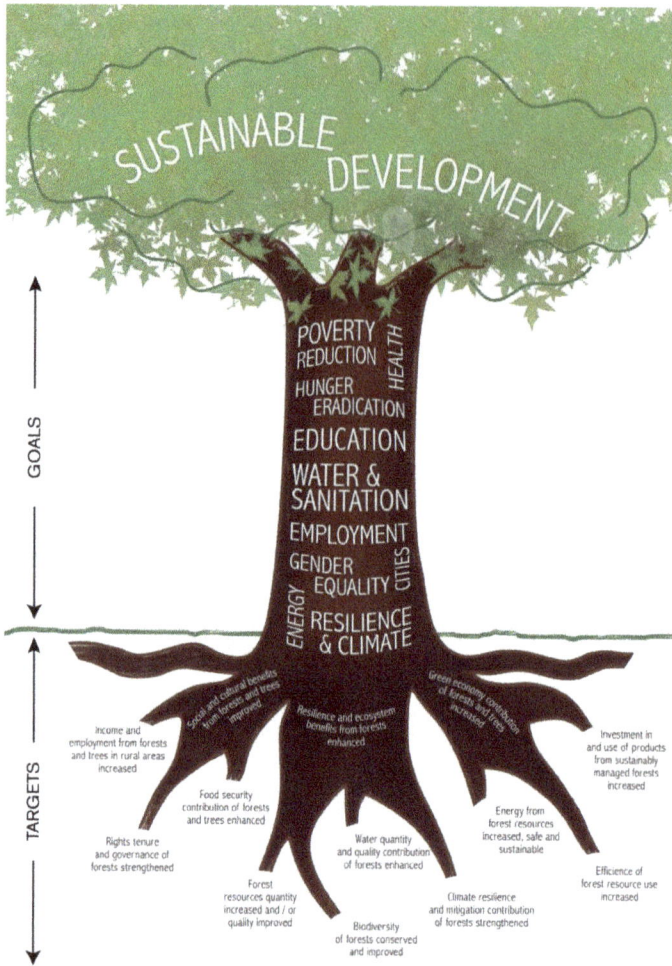

Figure 2.3 Key issues addressed by the 17 SDGs [10].

Unlike the MDGs, which relied exclusively on funding from governments and nonprofit organizations, the SDGs also rely on the private business sector to make contributions. The SDGs serve as a blueprint for peace and prosperity for people and the planet, now, and into the future. Every year, the UN Secretary General presents an annual SDG Progress report. Earth Council Alliance (ECA), network of nongovernmental organizations (NGOs) and individuals dedicated to promoting sustainable development, supports the sustainability goals.

Sustainable development at any scale can be challenging because of society's competing economic, social, and environmental needs. Some experts have criticized certain features of the concept, including [11]:

• It is a multidimensional concept and its interpretation and understanding is often content and context specific

• Its generality or vagueness, which has led to a great deal of debate over which forms or aspects of development qualify as "sustainable"

• Its lack of quantifiable or objectively measurable goals

• Its assumption of the inevitability and desirability of industrialization and economic development

• Its failure to ultimately prioritize human needs or environmental commitments, either of which may reasonably be considered more important in certain circumstances

2.5 CRITICAL AREAS OF IMPORTANCE

The SDGs are a call-to-action for people worldwide to address five critical areas of importance by 2030: people, planet, prosperity, peace, and partnership. This is displayed in Figure 2.4 [12] and explained as follows [13]:

Figure 2.4 The five dimensions of the 2030 Agenda [12].

1.   *People* - to end poverty and hunger, in all their forms and dimensions, and to ensure that all human beings can fulfill their potential in dignity and equality and in a healthy environment

2.   *Peace* - to foster peaceful, just and inclusive societies, which are free from fear and violence. There can be no sustainable development without peace and no peace without sustainable development.

3.   *Partnership* - to mobilize the means required to implement this Agenda through a revitalized Global Partnership for Sustainable Development, based on spirit of strengthened global solidarity, focused in particular on the needs of the poorest and most vulnerable and with the participation of all countries, all stakeholders and all people.

4.   *Prosperity* - to ensure that all human beings can enjoy prosperous and fulfilling lives and that economic, social and technological progress occur in harmony with nature.

5.   *Planet* - to protect the planet from degradation, including through sustainable consumption and production, sustainably managing its natural resources and taking urgent action on climate change, so that it can support the needs of the present and future generations.

2.6 APPLICATIONS OF SUSTAINABLE DEVELOPMENT

Sustainable development has become the catchphrase for international aid agencies, the jargon of development planners, and the slogan of development and environmental activists. It has attracted much attention in the academic, governance, planning, and development intervention space. Although the three pillars of sustainable development can apply to any business or industry, we will only consider its implications in the following areas.

•   *Human Development:* Proper human resource management and development is an important implication of social development. It is the people who have to ensure that the principles are adopted and adhered to. It is people who have the responsibility to utilize and conserve the environment. Sustainable development relates to the principle of meeting human development goals while at the same time sustaining the ability of natural systems to provide the natural resources and ecosystem services on which the economy and society depend. It implies human thinking and actions in the quest for sustainable human development. In order to achieve SD, there is the need for population control. There is also the need for all nations to formulate and implement social policies that foster tolerance, social cohesion, and justice. This can be done by enshrining universal human rights within a framework of citizenship, inclusion, equity, and effective political governance. UN should acknowledge and consider different national capacities and levels of development and respect national policies and priorities [14].

• *Sustainable City:* This is an urban center that improves its environmental impact through urban planning and management. You can imagine a city with parks and green spaces, solar-powered buildings, rooftop gardens, and more pedestrians and bicycles than cars. Smart cities are actively moving towards greener urban ecosystems and better environmental management [15].

• *Sustainable Urban Development:* This is characterized as achieving a balance between the development of and equity in the urban areas and the protection of the urban environment. Today, more than half of the world's population – 4.4 billion inhabitants – live in cities. Urban settlements, as a densely populated built environment, are the center of attention. The speed and scale of urbanization brings challenges. Cities play an increasingly important role in tackling climate change. Rapid population growth, economic development and a demand for more natural resources have put a strain on our planet. We must work hard to change the way we develop, maintain and dispose of our buildings. Figure 2.5 shows various elements of sustainable urban development [16].

Figure 2.5 Various elements of sustainable urban development [16]

• *Sustainable Construction:* This aims at applying the principles of sustainable development to the construction industry. It involves developing buildings such as houses, offices and other commercial properties that incorporate and use renewable and recyclable resources, with the primary goal of lessening the impact on the environment. It also entails supporting natural environments and habitats. Sustainable development affects different areas of construction, such as energy, technology, manufacturing and transport. As one of the biggest consumers of natural resources (such as water), the construction industry has a big part to play in sustainable development. Sustainable construction is crucial if we want to make developments work for ourselves, future generations, and the environment. We need to ensure the construction industry meets the needs of the current population while preserving the needs of future generations. The industry needs to shake off the reputation of being slow to adapt. Construction professionals should consider the impact transport has on the environment and make considered choices. A construction site is shown in Figure 2.6 [17].

Figure 2.6 Construction sustainability and technology [17].

- *Sustainable Forestry:* We cannot survive on this planet without forests. Forests provide fuel for cooking and warmth, medicinal plants, food, wildlife habitat, clean water, spiritual and cultural touchstones, and for many, the means to earn a living. Tearing forest down for materials like timber is not good for the environment. Look for companies that replace trees they plant or look for recycled materials if you want to go one better.

- *Corporate Social Responsibility:* This is a self-regulating business model that helps a company to be socially accountable to itself, its stakeholders, and the public. By practicing corporate social responsibility (CSR), companies can be conscious of the kind of impact they are having on all aspects of society, including economic, social, and environmental. Businesses must consider the interests of communities and the environment that they operate in. Businesses should not base their decisions solely on profit; other factors such as social and environmental should be considered.

2.7 BENEFITS

Sustainable development refers to policies, projects, and investments that provide benefits today without sacrificing environmental, social, and personal health in the future. The concept of sustainable development has emerged as a beacon of hope for our planet's future. Sustainable development charts a path towards a world where humans and nature coexist harmoniously. Where development is sustainable, everyone has access to decent work, quality health care, and education. Natural resource use avoids pollution and permanent losses to the environment. Public policy choices ensure that no one is left behind due to disadvantages or discrimination. As the threats of climate change become increasingly important, win-win strategies for mitigation, health improvement, and cost savings offer a range of advantages for various stakeholders. Other benefits of sustainable development include the following [12]:

1.   *Equity:* This refers to the accessibility and distribution of goods. Sustainable development gives importance on equity. Equity not only for the present generation but also equity for human generations yet to come. The sustainable development goals are a universal call to action to end poverty and social inequality while tackling climate change.

2.   *Economic Efficiency:* This helps maximize income. It is measured against the ideal of Pareto optimality, which encourages actions that will improve the welfare of at least one individual without worsening the situation of others.

3.   *Ethics:* There is an ethical dimension of sustainable development. Ethics demands harmonious integration between human and social development. When society as a whole is considered for sustainable development, ethical questions arise more powerfully. Ethical issues can motivate or discourage the leadership to adopt policies leading to sustainable development.

4.   *Politics:* Politics is related with achieving the goal of sustainable development. It deals with how to achieve the goal, from public policies and public policy making. We must engage in the political process and vote. We must also engage in dialogs, partnerships, and actions to work towards sustainability, inclusivity, and justice.

5.   *Culture:* This is generally regarded as a blueprint according to which the members of a society or a group go about their daily lives. Culture is a set of shared values, shared beliefs, and common expectations around which people organize their lives. Culture shapes and directs the will of the people. Society is culturally inhomogenous. It is made up of many small groups, called subcultures. There can be

conflict in subcultures. The prioritization of few groups over others in business, environmental protection, legislations can create inequality among subcultures. Sustainability calls for inclusion of interests of different subcultures.

6.   *Reduces Waste:* Making attempts to eliminate waste from your life can make a difference. Try buying fruits and vegetables locally. Donate your old clothes to charity.

7.   *Social Development:* This aims to attain the well-being of an individual and society at large. It entails the availability of necessary resources, proper healthcare, and good quality of life for people. SD aims to provide a method for rebuilding existing developments to make them eco-friendly facilities and projects.

8.   *Clean Energy:* This is sustainable and produces far less pollution than fossil fuels. If we want to become more sustainable, we need to increase the amount of clean energy we use and reduce the amount of fossil fuels. Clean energy starts with energy-efficient design: making the most of natural light, smart windows, and HVAC systems.

2.8 CHALLENGES

The concept of sustainable development has been criticized in various ways. Critics question what is to be sustained in sustainable development. Part of the problem is that "development" itself is not consistently defined. While some see it as an oxymoron and regard development as inherently unsustainable, others are disappointed in the lack of progress that has been achieved so far [15]. SDGs are not being accomplished at the appropriate speed needed to meet the 2030 deadline. The world is currently facing extremely difficult challenges to sustainable development. The food crisis, energy crisis, financial crisis, a global recession, and climate crisis are all interconnected and the only way of addressing them effectively is through integrated solutions. Other challenges of sustainable development include the following [18,19]:

1.   *Poverty Eradication:* Eradicating extreme poverty, promoting sustainable consumption and production, and managing the planet's natural resource for the benefit of all are the overarching challenges

of sustainable development. Poverty is the state for the majority of the world's people and nations. It is estimated that approximately 700 million people worldwide still live on less than US$1.90 per day, including a disproportionate number of women and people with disabilities. People live in poverty because of a range of factors— where they live, their ethnicity, gender, a lack of opportunities, and others. UNDP is looking at both inequalities and poverty in order to leave no one behind, focusing on the dynamics of exiting poverty. UNDP interventions help eradicate poverty, such as by creating decent jobs and livelihoods, providing social safety nets, boosting political participation, and ensuring access to services like water, energy, healthcare, credit, and productive assets. The global goal of halving poverty was achieved in 2010.

2.   *Climate Change:* Climate and sustainability have become measures of corporate performance. Some nations are severely affected by shocks and stressors such as climate change, disasters, conflict, insecurity, and environmental degradation. Climate-related disasters have increased in number and magnitude, contributing to social upheaval. Disasters and the effects of climate change have displaced more people than ever before.

3.   *Women Empowerment:* An important area of the SDGs that lacks progress is gender equality. Women's participation in all areas of society is important to making big and lasting changes. Women and girls make up a disproportionate share of people in poverty, and are more likely to face hunger, violence, and the impacts of disaster and climate change. UNDP is focusing on gender equality, the empowerment of women and girls, and meeting the needs of vulnerable groups, to ensure that no one is left behind. Countries were scored against SDGs targets that particularly affect women, such as access to safe water or the Internet. On a scale of 0 to 100, where a score of 100 means equality has been achieved. Denmark was the top performing country out of 129 countries with score slightly under 90.

4.   *Bad Governance:* Government transcends all sectors in a given society. Bad leadership produces bad governance or bad government. People's lives are better when government is efficient and responsive and people can aspire to a sustainable future with prosperity, peace, justice and security. When people from all social groups are included

in decision-making that affects their lives, and when they have equal access to fair institutions that provide services and administer justice, they will have more trust in their government. Food, shelter, clean air, education, and opportunities for the people depend on having a good governance. Leaders must be aligned, committed, and supported if they are to demonstrate new behaviors.

5.   *People Engagement:* It is not only up to our political leaders. Every person can benefit from a more prosperous, inclusive and resilient world. We can all do something about it, regardless of our position, in the government, business, school or home. People are at the center of any change effort and they must be engaged. Leaders need to make sure the entire workforce is engaged and committed. Working with the right people will get you on the right track.

6.   *Brain Drain:* This is a major problem for many developing nations that lose their skilled workers to richer countries. Reasons for this brain drain vary, ranging from poor conditions domestically to attractive opportunities and active enticement from abroad. For example, many medical doctors leave Sub-Sahara African and migrate to United States, United Kingdom, Europe, and Canada.

7.   *Rapid Urbanization:* In developing countries in particular, rapid urbanization calls for major changes in the way in which urban development is designed and managed. Today, over 50% of the world population already live in cities and urban areas. Rapid urbanization is exerting pressure on fresh water supplies, sewage, the living environment, and public health. Major urban challenges are shown in Figure 2.7 [20].

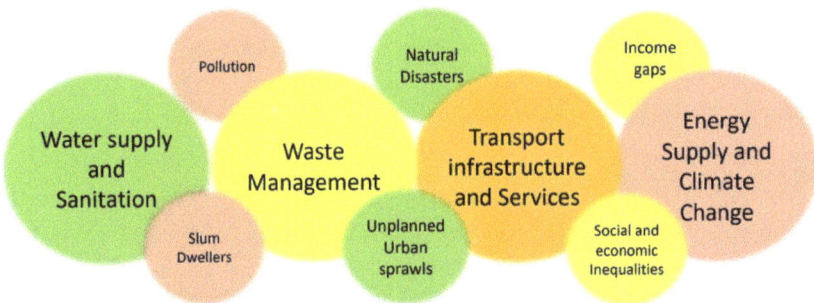

Figure 2.7 Major urban challenges [20]

8. *Affordable Energy:* People cannot prosper without reliable, safe, and affordable energy to power everything from lights to factories. Energy is connected to every one of the SDGs. UNDP helps countries transition away from the use of finite fossil fuels and towards clean, renewable, affordable sources of energy.

9. *Industrialisation:* This has had a rippling effect on this planet's environment. It is responsible for numerous environmental issues, among which foremost is the depletion of resources along with deforestation. Industrial waste often contains toxic materials and have been greatly responsible for pollution with effects like water pollution, air pollution, and noise pollution. Crucial to the transition is a rapid phase out of coal, primarily in its use for electricity generation and industrial sectors.

10. *Globalization:* This has provided opportunities for emerging economies and developing nations. In the nineteenth century, the world economy underwent its first process of globalization. Today's globalization is therefore not entirely unprecedented in terms of trade levels, but it is qualitatively different. Beyond the mere expansion of trade and investment flows, underlying global production patterns have changed in recent decades. Globalization has progressed in finance, where the liberalization of capital markets and short-term capital flows have been promoted by the International Monetary Fund (IMF) since the 1980s.

2.9 CONCLUSION

The world is faced with challenges in all three dimensions of sustainable development—economic, social, and environmental. More than 1 billion people are still living in extreme poverty, and income inequality within and among many countries has been rising. Unsustainable consumption and production patterns have resulted in huge economic and social costs and may endanger life on the planet. Sustainable development is a development that meets the needs of the present without compromising the ability of future generations to meet their own needs. It aims at making use of natural resources and the environment for improving the standard of people in such a way that the ability of future generations to meet their own needs is not compromised. It attempts to find a balance between economic development, environmental protection, and social well-being. More needs to be done by the key players—particularly the United Nations, governments, private sector, and civil society organizations to ensure that everyone is sustainable development aware, conscious, cultured, and compliant.

Sustainable development is how we must live today if we want a better tomorrow. The goals of the sustainable development project cannot and will not be met without the help of everyone. As illustrated in Figure 2.8, a better future is possible if we all act now [21].

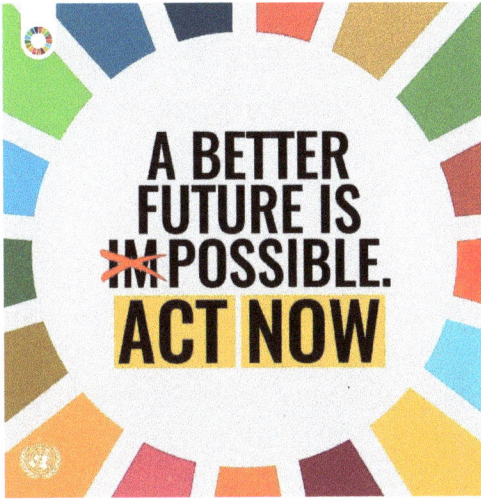

Figure 2.8 A better future is possible if we act now [21]

There are many actions, big and small, that the average person can take to contribute to sustainable development. Boosting your knowledge and taking a class may help you learn about climate change. Eliminating waste can make a difference. Taking the bus or train is typically cheaper and better for the environment than driving a car. Save on electricity at home by unplugging appliances when not in use. Opt for online paperless statements instead of having bills mailed to you. Consider a career in sustainable development. Sustainable development encompasses many broad fields, such as management, public policy, law, urban planning, education, etc. So there are plenty of jobs you can choose from. For more information on sustainable development, one should consult books in [22-45] and the following related journals:

- *Sustainability.*

- *Sustainable Development*

- *Journal of Sustainable Development*

- *International Journal of Sustainable Development and Planning*

- *International Journal of Sustainable Development and World Ecology*

- *Indian Journal of Sustainable Development*

- *Asia Pacific Sustainable Development Journal*

REFERENCE

[1]   M. N. O. Sadiku, P. A. Adekunte, and J. O. Sadiku, "Sustainable development: A primer," International Journal of Trend in Scientific Research and Development, vol. 8, no. 1, January-February 2024, pp.425-433.

[2]   "What is sustainable development and why is it necessary?" August 2023,

https://utopia.org/guide/what-is-sustainable-development-and-why-is-it-necessary/

[3]   T. Kuhlman and J. Farrington, "What is sustainability?" Sustainability, vol. 2, 2010, pp. 3436-3448.

[4]   A. Browne, "Explainer: What is sustainability and why is it important?" October 2022,

https://earth.org/what-is-sustainability/

[5]   "What is sustainability?"

https://www.mcgill.ca/sustainability/files/sustainability/what-is-sustainability.pdf

[6]   S. R. Elliot, "Sustainability: an economic perspective," Resources, Conservation and Recycling, vol. 44, no. 3, June 2005, pp. 263-277.

[7]   "What is sustainable development?"

https://envirotaqa.com/sustainable-development/

[8]   "Sustainable development: Goals, importance, and career guide," November 2023,

https://www.coursera.org/articles/sustainable-development

[9]   "Sustainable Development Goals,"

https://education.nationalgeographic.org/resource/sustainable-development-goals/

[10]   https://www.pinterest.nz/pin/798192733934359652/

[11]   "Department of Economic and Social Affairs Sustainable Development," Unknown Source.

[12]   "A 360° view on sustainable development,"May 2018,

https://cpd.org.bd/a-general-outline-of-evolution-of-ngo-and-development-work-in-bd-part-vi/

[13]   O. Olayide, "Introduction to the Sustainable Development Goals," October 2016,

https://www.researchgate.net/publication/312835158_Introduction_to_the_Sustainable_Development_Goals

[14]   J. Mensah, "Sustainable development: Meaning, history, principles, pillars, and implications for human action: Literature review," Cogent Social Sciences, vol, 5, no.1, 2019.

[15]   "Sustainable development," Wikipedia, the free encyclopedia https://en.wikipedia.org/wiki/Sustainable_development

[16]   https://www.researchgate.net/figure/Sustainable-urban-development-a-synthesis-framework-with-three-dimensions-and-ten-themes_fig4_303379673

[17]   "Sustainable and construction: What you need to know,"

https://www.letsbuild.com/blog/sustainable-construction-what-you-need-to-know

[18]   "Development challenges and solutions,"

https://www.undp.org/development-challenges-and-solutions

[19]   S. Santamarta et al., "The challenges of a sustainability transformation," July 2022,

https://www.bcg.com/publications/2022/the-challenges-of-a-sustainability-transformation

[20] C. Takase, "Implementing SDG 11 – key elements, challenges and opportunities,"

https://sustainabledevelopment.un.org/content/unosd/

documents/4057Module%204%20SDG%2011_Chicako%20Takase.

pdf

[21] "Fast facts – What is sustainable development?"
https://www.un.org/sustainabledevelopment/blog/2023/08/what-is-sustainable-development/

[22] M. F. Ashby, Michael F. Materials and Sustainable Development. Butterworth-Heinemann, 2022.

[23] J. Blewitt, Understanding Sustainable Development. Routledge, 2012.

[24] M. Carley and I. Christie, Managing Sustainable Development. Routledge, 2017.

[25] H. E. Daly, Beyond Growth: The Economics of Sustainable Development. Beacon Press, 2014.

[26] J. Elliott, An Introduction to Sustainable Development. Routledge, 2012.

[27] A. Espinosa and J. Walker, Complexity Approach to Sustainability, A: Theory and Application. World Scientific, 2017.

[28] G. C. Gallopín, A Systems Approach to Sustainability and Sustainable Development. ECLAC, 2003.

[29] I. Goldin and L. A. Winters (eds.), The Economics of Sustainable Development. Cambridge University Press, 1995.

[30] N. E. Harrison, Constructing Sustainable Development. Suny Press, 2000.

[31] M. Mawhinney, Sustainable Development: Understanding the Green Debates. John Wiley & Sons, 2008.

[32] N. Middleton and P. O'Keefe, Redefining Sustainable Development. London: Pluto Press, 2001.

[33] I. Moffatt, N. Hanley, and M. D. Wilson, Measuring and Modelling: Sustainable Development. Parthenon Publishing Group Inc., 2001.

[34] I. Moffatt, Sustainable Development: Principles, Analysis and Policies. Parthenon Publishing Group, 1996.

[35]   M. Redclift, Sustainable Development: Exploring the Contradictions. Routledge, 2002.

[36]   D. Reid, Sustainable Development: An Introductory Guide. Routledge, 2013.

[37]   P. P. Rogers, K. F. Jalal, and J. A. Boyd, An Introduction to Sustainable Development. Earthscan, 2012.

[38]   N. Roorda, Fundamentals of Sustainable Development. Routledge, 2020.

[39]   J. D. Sachs, The Age of Sustainable Development. Columbia University Press, 2015.

[40]   J. D. Sachs et al., Sustainable Development Report 2022. Cambridge University Press, 2022.

[41]   J. Sayer and B. Campbell, The Science of Sustainable Development. Cambridge University Press, Cambridge, UK, 2004.

[42]   T. P. Soubbotina, Beyond Economic Growth: An Introduction to Sustainable Development. World Bank Publications, 2004.

[43]   G. Atkinson et al. (eds.), Handbook of Sustainable Development. Edward Elgar Publishing, 2014.

[44]   S. Bass, B. Dalal-Clayton, and J. Pretty, Participation in Strategies for Sustainable Development. London: IIED, 1995.

[45]   S. Beder, The Nature of Sustainable Development. Newham: Scribe Publications, 1996.

CHAPTER 3
SUSTAINABLE CITIES

"Cities can be the engine of social equity and economic opportunity. They can help us reduce our carbon footprint and protect the global environment. That is why it is so important that we work together to build the capacity of mayors and all those concerned in planning and running sustainable cities."

– Ban Ki-moon

3.1 INTRODUCTION

Today, people are living longer than ever before. The sheer number of people who live in cities now is massive. The majority of the world is now urban and the world is becoming increasingly urbanized. Half of the world's population (3.5 billion people) now lives in cities. By 2050, it is predicted that 70 per cent of the world population will be in urban settlements. This rapid urbanization is exerting pressure on fresh water supplies, sewage, living environment, public health, traffic, waste production, and overall quality of life. It is resulting in a growing number of slum dwellers, inadequate, and overburdened infrastructure, uncontrolled urban growth, congested traffic, a worsening air pollution, environmental degradation, inadequate urban infrastructure, and a lack of basic services, such as water supply, sanitation, and waste management, all of which increase the vulnerability of cities to natural disasters [1]. Balancing the immediate needs of today without sacrificing the demands of tomorrow is at the heart of sustainability.

Cities are increasingly connected to each other economically, socially, and culturally. Although each city is unique, they share a great number of common expectations. Megacities typically concentrate large proportions of the economic, environmental, and human resources of their nations. Human capital development, attractions of sustainable living standards, and renewed concerns for the planet have refocused city planners to a new frontier: the creation of sustainable cities [2].

By nature, humans are social creatures and thrive in urban spaces that foster social connections. Cities are essential to sustainable development since they are the center of economic development. They interact extensively with surrounding and with the rest of the world. The sustainable city concept focuses on improving the conditions of the urban areas in order to create healthy, pleasant, livable, inclusive, safe, and resilient cities where residents want to live and work [3].

This chapter provides an introduction on sustainable cities. It begins with explaining what sustainable cities are all about. It provides United Nations' Sustainable Development Goals (SDGs), which are vital for developing sustainable cities. It specifies how to create sustainable cities. It provides applications and examples of sustainable cities. It highlights the benefits and challenges of sustainable cities. The last section concludes with comments.

3.2 WHAT ARE SUSTAINABLE CITIES?

The idea of sustainable cities came out of an understanding of the importance of individual human behavior. Sustainability is often defined as meeting the needs of the current generation without compromising the ability for future generations to meet those same needs. To achieve sustainability, we must think about how to implement it in all facets of life: buildings, streets, parks, roads, sidewalks, etc. Cities are key to sustainable development and sustainable future. They are responsible for making policies that affect sustainability.

A sustainable city, also referred to as an eco-city, is a city designed with consideration for the triple bottom line: social, economic, environmental impact, as illustrated in Figure 3.1 [4].

Figure 3.1 Sustainable development [4].

It is one in which its people and businesses continuously endeavor to improve their natural, built, and cultural environments. For a city to be sustainable, all of those parts must be sustainable as well. Thus, sustainable city must have sustainable shelter markets, sustainable development, sustainable transport, sustainable agriculture, sustainable livelihoods, sustainable resource use, sustainable water supply, sustainable production/manufacturing, sustainable energy use, etc.

Socially sustainable cities should be equitable, diverse, inclusive, connected, democratic, and provide a good quality of life. While creating sustainable living conditions for all its inhabitants, a sustainable city should also promote economic growth and meet their basic needs. Sustainable cities should promote sustainable developments and encourage people to live in a more sustainable and environmentally-friendly way. They facilitate economic production and consumption processes while reducing our impact on the natural world.

The main characteristics of a sustainable city include [5]:

• It introduces greenery into the urban environment to reduce CO_2 emissins and improve the quality of its air.

• It promotes renewable energies to conserve and protect natural resources.

• It successfully implement sustainable mobility and the use of public transport, and is committed to a circular economy.

• It will grow at a sustainable rate and use resources in a sustainable way.

• Resources and services in the city are accessible to all.

• Public transport is seen as a viable alternative to cars.

• Public transport is safe and reliable.

• Walking and cycling is safe.

• Wherever possible, renewable resources are used instead of non-renewable resources.

• Waste is seen as a resource and is recycled wherever possible.

• There is access to affordable housing.

• Community links are strong and communities work together to deal with issues such as crime and security.

Smart sustainable cities (SSC) is an aggregate concept that combines smart cities and sustainable cities, as shown in Figure 3.2. Cities can be made sustainable without the use of smart (ICT) technology, and smart technologies can be used in cities without contributing to sustainable development [6].

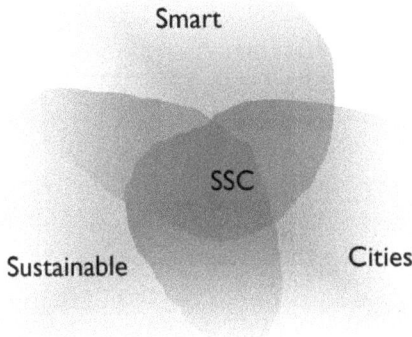

Figure 3.2 Smart sustainable cities (SSC) [6].

A smart sustainable city is an innovative city that uses ICTs and other means to improve quality of life, efficiency of urban operation and services and competitiveness. ICTs can leverage artificial intelligence (AI) and other technologies to further our understanding of urbanization, thereby providing useful information to tackle urban challenges and minimize climate risks.

Another concept related to cities is "green growth," which refers to economic growth that not only preserves but enhances the inherited natural resources. A green city is a city that is focused on sustainability. Building a green city is somewhat equivalent to the building of sustainability [7]. Green spaces are increasingly becoming part of the efforts to promote sustainability because of the different areas of benefits they provided. Implementing green policies at the local level typically confronts some problems.

3.3 SUSTAINABLE DEVELOPMENT GOALS

Nations and organizations worldwide have determined to work together and achieve the United Nations' Sustainable Development Goals (SDGs). United Nations Environment Programme (UNEP) assists member states and organizations to achieve relevant SDGs on cities including SDG 11 (sustainable cities and human settlements). The SDG 11 defines sustainable cities as those that are dedicated to achieving green sustainability, social sustainability, and economic sustainability. Sustainable development goals (SDGs) are regarded as extension of Millennium Development Goals (MDGs) and a post-2015 agenda to fight against poverty and eradicate human deprivation [8].

The 2030 Sustainable Development Agenda is applicable to all nations and goes well beyond the MDGs. The Sustainable Development Goals (SDGs) comprise a broad range of economic, social, and environmental objectives, and offer the prospect of more peaceful and inclusive societies. They comprise of 17 goals and 169 targets. The goals are illustrated in Figure 3.3 [9] and stated as follows [10]:

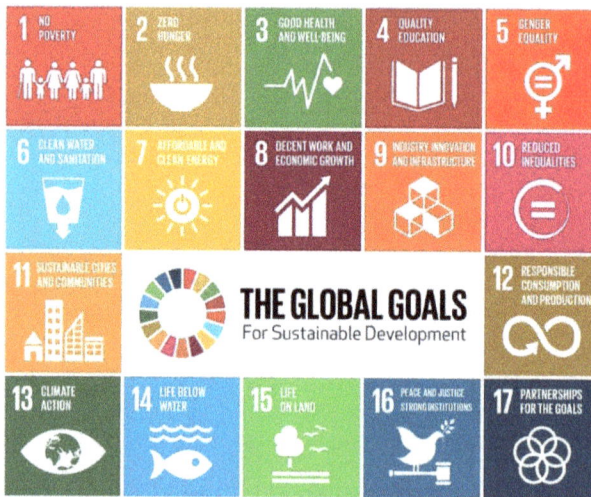

Figure 3.3 Seventeen Sustainable Development Goals [9].

1.   End poverty in all its forms everywhere.

2.   End hunger, achieve food security and improved nutrition and promote sustainable agriculture.

3.   Ensure healthy lives and promote well-being for all at all ages.

4.   Ensure inclusive and equitable quality education and promote lifelong learning opportunities for all.

5.   Achieve gender equality and empower all women and girls.

6. Ensure availability and sustainable management of water and sanitation for all.

7. Ensure access to affordable, reliable, sustainable, and modern energy for all.

8. Promote sustained, inclusive and sustainable economic growth, full and productive employment and decent work for all.

9. Build resilient infrastructure, promote inclusive and sustainable industrialization and foster innovation.

10. Reduce inequality within and among countries.

11. Make cities and human settlements inclusive, safe, resilient, and sustainable.

12. Ensure sustainable consumption and production patterns.

13. Take urgent action to combat climate change and its impacts.

14. Conserve and sustainably use the oceans, seas, and marine resources for sustainable development.

15. Protect, restore, and promote sustainable use of terrestrial ecosystems, sustainably manage forests, combat desertification, and halt and reverse land degradation and halt biodiversity loss.

16. Promote peaceful and inclusive societies for sustainable development, provide access to justice for all and build effective, accountable and inclusive institutions at all levels.

17. Strengthen the means of implementation and revitalize the global partnership for sustainable development.

While poverty eradication and food security remain priorities, the Sustainable Development Goals (SDGs) comprise a broad range of economic, social, and environmental objectives. In contrast to the MDGs, the SDGs are uniformly applicable to all countries of the world, removing the "developing" versus "developed" dichotomy that left the MDGs open to criticism. Critics of the new SDGs complain that the goals are too many. As illustrated in Figure 3.4, partnerships among governments, private sector, and other civil society groups can help achieve sustainable lifestyles and spur new businesses with additional jobs focusing on green technologies and environmental services [1].

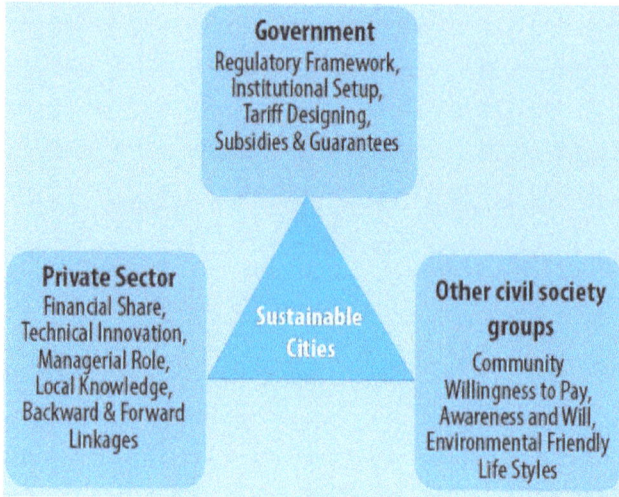

Figure 3.4 Partnership in developing sustainable cities [1].

3.4 CREATING SUSTAINABLE CITIES

Sustainable cities reduce the environmental impact and increase resilience through various means including [11]:

• Urban farming is the process of growing and distributing food, as well as raising animals, in and around a city. This reduces the distance food has to travel from field to fork.

• Renewable energy sources, such as wind turbines, solar panels, or bio-gas created from sewage to reduce and manage pollution.

• Various methods to reduce the need for air conditioning (a massive energy demand), such as planting trees and lightening surface colors, natural ventilation systems, an increase in water features, and green spaces equaling at least 20% of the city's surface.

• Improved public transport and an increase in pedestrianization to reduce car emissions. This requires a radically different approach to city planning, with integrated business, industrial, and residential zones.

• Optimal building density to make public transport viable but avoid the creation of urban heat islands.

• Green roofs alter the surface energy balance and can help mitigate the urban heat island effect. Incorporating eco roofs or green roofs in your design will help with air quality, climate, and water runoff.

• Zero-emission transport

• Zero-energy building

• Sustainable urban drainage systems or SUDS in addition to other systems to reduce and manage waste.

• Solutions to decrease urban sprawl, by seeking new ways of allowing people to live closer to the workspace.

• Educating residents of cities about the importance and positive impacts of living in a more sustainable city.

• Policy and planning changes to meet the unmet demands for urban services (water, energy, transport).

• A building should become LEED (Leadership in Energy and Environmental Design) certified. LEED recognizes whole building sustainable design by identifying key areas of excellence including: Sustainable Sites, Water Efficiency, Energy and Atmosphere, Materials and Resources, Indoor Environmental Quality, Locations & Linkages, Awareness and Education, Innovation in Design, Regional Priority.

• Sustainable transportation attempts to reduce a city's reliance and use of greenhouse emitting gases by utilizing low environmental impact vehicles. Poor transportation systems lead to traffic jams and high levels of pollution.

3.5 APPLICATIONS OF SUSTAINABLE CITIES

As cities grow, many of their inhabitants gain opportunities, prosperity, and well-being, but that growth also significantly upsets the social, economic, and environmental balance. Sustainability of cities requires that the living conditions and activities within urban areas are "sustainable," i.e. sustainable shelter markets, sustainable development, sustainable transport, sustainable construction, sustainable infrastructure, sustainable agriculture, sustainable livelihoods, sustainable resource use, sustainable water supply, sustainable production/manufacturing, sustainable energy use, etc. [12]. Thus sustainability in cities is demonstrated in the following applications.

• *Sustainable Infrastructure:* Cities that focus on sustainability must address infrastructure head-on. A city's infrastructure consists of roads, airports, hospitals, subways and railway systems, water utilities, power and telecommunications grids, etc. The delivery, operation, and management of infrastructure is the lifeblood of any economy. There is a growing need to transform how infrastructure is planned, delivered, and managed as urbanization, digitalization, and climate change increasingly impact the world. Sustainable infrastructure refers to equipment and systems that are designed to meet the population's essential service needs, including highways, bridges, telephone systems, power systems, etc., based on all-round sustainable principles. This means the infrastructure is environmentally friendly from end to end, and that includes economic, financial, social, and institutional factors. Sustainable infrastructure will require a change in how construction projects are planned, delivered, and managed. Sustainable infrastructure is showing its worth as a more efficient, productive, and environmentally friendly option [13,14]. As cities evolve over time, city planners are trying to implement more environmentally friendly infrastructure.

• *Sustainable Construction:* It is the practice of creating structures and using processes that are environmentally responsible and resource-efficient throughout a building's lifecycle. It involves the introduction of healthy living and workplace environments, the use of materials that are sustainable, durable, and environmentally friendly. Sustainable construction focuses on six principles: conserve, reuse, recycle/renew, protect nature, create nontoxic and high quality. It is the use of renewable and recyclable materials in construction to reduce energy consumption and wastage. The construction industry sits between a rock and a hard place. The earth's urbanizing, growing population is placing enormous demands on the construction sector. By conservative estimates, the construction industry is responsible for more than 30% of the world's natural-resource extraction and a quarter of the solid waste generated [15].

• *Sustainable Transportation:* The growth of speedy transportation is man's greatest achievement in minimizing distances, but at the same time it has also become a cause of environmental degradation. The environmental implications of transport development have become very widely recognized. Environmental concerns and limited parking space have forced cities to rethink their transportation infrastructure. Sustainable transportation or mobility refers to the use of environmentally-friendly modes of transportation that minimize negative impacts on the environment and promote social equity . It includes options such as public transit, cycling, walking, and carpooling, as well as the use of fuel-efficient and electric vehicles. The benefits of sustainable transportation include reduced greenhouse gas emissions, improved air quality, reduced traffic congestion, and cost savings on fuel and vehicles. The United States Department of Energy has been promoting sustainable transportation through research and development of low- and zero-emission, energy-efficient, and affordable modes of transport, including electric and alternative-fuel vehicles, as well as domestic fuels. Sustainable transportation is central to sustainable cities, with its objectives of universal access, enhanced safety, reduced environmental and climate impact, improved resilience, and greater efficiency. Sustainable transport systems make a positive contribution to the environmental, social, and economic sustainability of the communities they serve. The future of transportation is tackling greener public transit [16].

• *Green Buildings:* Green building design is becoming popular as more owners feel a responsibility to build sustainably. Green building consists of water recycling, solar power installations, cooling systems, and energy efficient window systems. It provides greener solutions to normal building processes that conserve water, save energy, and provide cleaner indoor air, while also reducing utility bills. It is designed to independently use renewable energy. The main benefit of building green is reducing a building's impact on the environment and significantly improving building performance.

Using green technologies in building construction not only benefits the environment, but they can produce economically attractive buildings that are healthier for the occupants as well. Using green roofs improved the energy performance of buildings because they provide higher thermal inertia, shading, and absorption of solar energy. Green buildings have the potential to substantially reduce energy consumption. They will become a new trend in the future [17]. The benefits of green buildings are displayed in Figure 3.5 [18].

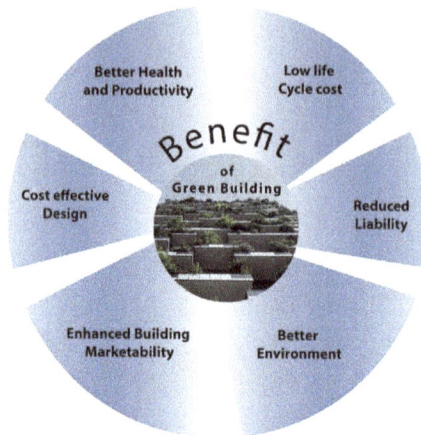

Source: Internet

Figure 3.5 The benefits of a green building [18].

• *Urban Farms:* Food is second to energy as the most in-demand city resource. Urban farming enhances food production, reduces food insecurity, and mitigates the environmental effects of food transportation. The switch to clean energy is essential for cities to become sustainable. Urban farming is one way cities can cut down on carbon emissions tied to food production. Solar farms can improve air quality in a city while also providing renewable energy to citizens and municipal facilities. City-funded solar farms allow residents who cannot harness solar energy on their own property to gain access to solar power. It also allows municipal buildings to transition to renewable energy [19]. Vertical gardens have gained popularity in recent years as well. Figure 3.6 shows a typical urban farm [20].

Figure 3.6 A typical urban farm [20].

3.6 EXAMPLES OF SUSTAINABLE CITIES

The Arcadis Sustainable Cities Index ranks 100 global cities on three sustainability factors or pillars:

- *Profit:* The profit factor measures the value of real estate and the ease of starting and running businesses.

- *People:* The people index focuses on the living standard of the people, literacy, education, and health.

- *Planet:* The planet factor focuses on transportation, water, sanitation, air pollution, and carbon emission among other factors.

Here we consider some examples of ranked cities that have become leaders in sustainable development [12,21,22].

1. *San Francisco, California:* Focusing on technologies to improve energy efficiency in buildings and enhance its transportation system has made San Francisco a leader in sustainability. San Francisco came out tops when measured against key performance indicators across five categories: environmental quality, economic security, governance and empowerment, infrastructure and energy, and social well-being. San Francisco and the surrounding Bay Area constitute a

home to highly innovative companies in the world, such as Salesforce, Uber, and Twitter. Its streets are known for hybrid-electric buses and light rails with zero-emission. Advances in sustainable food, recycling, and composting will help San Francisco reach its goal of becoming zero waste by 2020. The local authorities are pushing forward bans on certain products that are causing damage to the environment. The city has mandated that garages and parking lots install EV charging stations for over 10% of their spaces.

2.　　*Copenhagen, Denmark:* This is one of the cities leading the sustainable revolution. This is often ranked as one of the greenest cities on the world. Copenhagen has focused on reducing energy consumption, reducing emissions, improving the health of its residents, integrating transport, and building "super cycle highways." In Copenhagen, bicycles outnumber cars by over 5:1, and nearly half the population commutes by bike.

3.　　*Vancouver, Canada:* Most cities in Canada have sustainability action plans which are easily downloaded from city websites. Vancouver is regarded as a perfect city to visit and live in due to its surroundings of ocean, forest and mountains. It is determined to be one of the greenest and most climate change resilient cities on earth. In 2002, Vancouver released the Greenest City Action Plan, which set 10 goals to be achieved by 2020. The goals include increasing green jobs, reducing community-based greenhouse gas emissions, and expanding green buildings around the city, getting 100 percent of its energy (including electricity, heating, cooling, and transport) from renewable sources by 2050, and striving for zero waste.

4.　　*Singapore:* This is the most sustainable city in Asia and the second in the world overall. The city-state is also dubbed "the garden city;" it has a population of roughly five million people. It is a self-governing city-state and an island nation. It has developed a Sustainable Development Blueprint with the goal of improving energy efficiency, ensuring its buildings are certified green, and having households live within a 10-minute walk to a train station. Singapore has also improved its sustainability by building effective public transportation systems, which has helped reduce pollution and crowding on streets. The government has focused on improving mobility and connectivity within the city.

5.   *Adelaide, South Australia:* The city launched an urban forest initiative in 2003 to plant 3 million native trees and shrubs by 2014 on 300 project sites include parks, reserves, transport corridors, schools, water courses, and coastline. The local government launched an initiative for Adelaide to lead Australia in the take-up of solar power. The government also embraced a Zero Waste recycling strategy. In the 1970s container deposit legislation was introduced. In 2010 Zero Waste SA was commended by a UN Habitat Report entitled "Solid Waste Management in the World Cities."

6.   *Cape Town, South Africa:* This city has been performing exceptionally well from an eco-friendly perspective and has made it to number seven on this list. It is one of the most innovative cities as far sustainability is concerned. The city has set an aim to get 10% of its energy from renewable sources and have 10% of homes running on solar energy by 2020.

7.   *Frankfurt, Germany:* This is the financial hub of Germany, hosting the European Central Bank. In 2000, Frankfurt committed to becoming the most sustainable city on Earth. Frankfurt has also been an eco-city for years. Frankfurt has been crowned with a major green belt that is home to 200,000 trees. Over 52% of Frankfurt is covered by open green spaces like water bodies, woodlands, and parks. The local government has a concrete plan for nature and water conservation, energy efficiency, and climate protection. Figure 3.7 shows the city-state of Frankfurt [23].

Figure 3.7 The city of Frankfurt [23].

8.   *New York:* The Big Apple is one of the most advanced cities for sustainability. It is implementing multiple sustainability programs. It dedicates 27% of its total land to green spaces, making it the highest ranking in the US. New York City now has over 550 community gardens.

This is an ever-changing list. The other ranked cities include London, Amsterdam, Hong Kong, Sydney, Los Angeles, Chicago, Zurich, Seoul, Frankfurt, and Dubai.

3.7 BENEFITS

Cities are engines of economic growth that have lifted millions from poverty. They offer an opportunity to integrate operations of systems of water, energy, transport, health, education, and security services. A sustainable city is one designed to address social, environmental, and economic impact through urban planning and city management. Many nations are adopting sustainability practices, as evident in new sustainable cities initiatives that are being launched. The priorities of a sustainable city include the ability to feed itself and the ability to power itself with renewable sources of energy, with more cyclists and pedestrians than cars. They will promote the use of public transit, walkability, and biking which would benefit citizens' health and the environment. They should also promote a great people climate that appeals to individuals and families of all types and create conditions under which humans can prosper [2]. Other benefits of sustainable cities include the following [24]:

1.   *Economic Benefits:* If managed well, sustainable cities can become drivers of the economy, contributing to local livability, global environmental benefits, and global public goods. Although cities are often characterized by stark socioeconomic inequalities and poor environmental conditions, they also offer growth and development potential. Urbanization has facilitated economic growth through productivity gains in the use of labor and capital. By concentrating people and economic activities, cities have some unique advantages. They have been the drivers of the economy and have lifted millions out of poverty.

2.   *Smart Cities:* These are actively moving toward greener urban ecosystems and better environmental stewardship. Smart cities are creating sustainable places with clean technology, parks and pathways, and urban sustainability principles. Green tech also supports green living practices, including recycling and use of energy and renewable resources in homes and offices. A sustainable city concept incorporates eco-friendly practices, green spaces and supporting technology into the urban environment to reduce air pollution and CO_2 emissions, enhance air quality, and protect natural resources. The components of smart city are shown in Figure 3.8 [25].

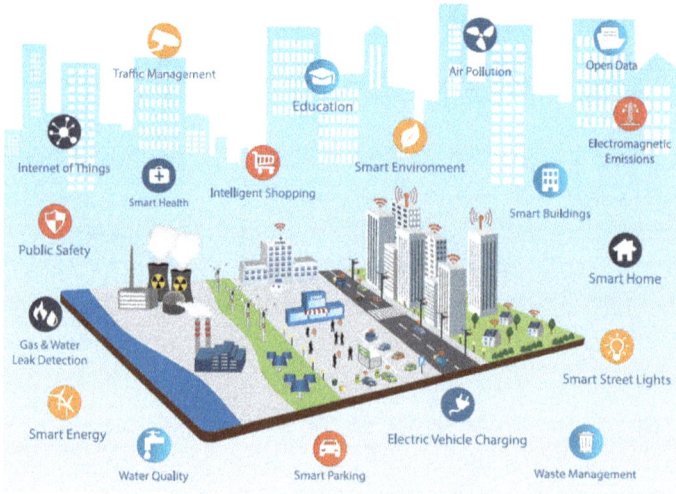

Figure 3.8 The components of a smart city [25]

3.   *Waste Management:* Cities can improve waste management through sustainable urban planning. Waste disposal processes can shift toward a circular economy model, and sustainable city waste management. Programs to minimize waste by recycling, composting, and repurposing materials are some proven ways cities can be more sustainable with waste management. This leads to reduced waste, and the energy used to manage it. For example, Dubai is powered by clean energy produced by recycling water and waste, and has banned single-use plastic bags.

4.   *Green Technology:* This is the key to a sustainable future. Green technology deals with using science and technology to protect the environment as well as curb the negative impacts of human involvement. It is any mode of technology that lovers CO_2 emissions. Some people refer to green technology as sustainable technology, environmental technology, or clean technology. Here green technology is used to mean effort to promote sustainability and reduce greenhouse gas emissions. Green technology is developed in response to a challenge that humankind faces. The top ten problems/challenges as follows: (1) energy, (2) water, (3) food, (4) environment, (5) poverty, (6) terrorism and war, (7) disease, (8) education, (9) democracy, and (10) population. Green technologies include green energy, green chemistry, green engineering, green IT, green food, green manufacturing, green

business, green economics, green supply chain, green logistics, green building, and green nanotechnology. Several business establishments have used at least one green technology or practice in order to make their production processes more environmentally friendly [26].

5.   *Urban Sustainability:* This is the concept of cities or urban areas equipped to be self-sufficient, in terms of energy requirements, water supply, and sanitation facilities, distribution of resources, food, etc. With an increasing world population, urban areas demand significant energy, materials, food and water, products, services, and human capital. Urbanization poses considerable challenges, including overpopulation, climate change, environmental quality, and access to energy. The importance of sustainable cities and communities is becoming increasingly vital in the quest to reverse environmental damage and improve the livability of cities. Urban centers are regarded to be the "growth drivers" of the future, where technology is expected to play a huge role. Urban areas should be able to produce their own energy preferably using renewable resources, reducing the amount of pollution generated. There should also be efficient use of land, along with efficient waste management.

6.   *Social Justice:* In recent years, the sustainability movement has shifted toward ensuring that adequate emphasis is given to social justice concerns, and to ensuring that we do not protect profits, or even the planet, at the expense of people or social equity. Environmentally conscious organizations are committed to creating an environmentally sound, socially just, and economically sustainable culture. The cities of the future may prioritize equality and justice.

Some of these benefits are illustrated in Figure 3.9 [27].

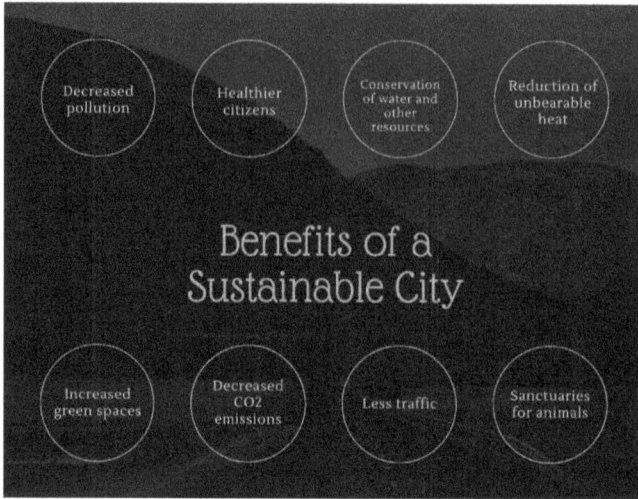

Figure 3.9 Some of these benefits of a sustainable city [27]

3.8 CHALLENGES

Despite the progress made on sustainable development, many challenges still exist that might hinder the SDG11 implementation process. Sceptics are of the opinion that there is little that a single city can do to achieve sustainability. There is no certainty about what sustainable cities might mean in practice. Maintaining economic growth, while creating sustainable livable cities for all, is the biggest urban challenge in most nations. Cities are finding it difficult to be livable and economically strong. Cities around the world are not balancing the pillars of sustainability. No city has truly balanced people, profit, and the planet. In spite of the good done by groups and individuals in favor of a better world, deterioration at all levels continues to increase at alarming rate. Dealing with the main urban challenges of the 21st century (climate change, resource depletion, rapid urbanization, poverty, etc.) becomes increasingly complex. Unfortunately, there are still countless mayors and city planners that do not have the capability or the will to instill change. Other challenges include the following [28-30].

1. *Climate Change:* This has unquestionably become the biggest global risk. With climate change looming over the planet, cities are doing what they can to become sustainable. We can hope that

individuals and organizations will do everything in their power to combat climate change. Sustainable cities are becoming essential in the quest to reverse global climate change. The development of sustainable cities is a lofty goal for authorities and city planners but paramount for combating climate change. Cities play an increasingly decisive role in actions to address climate and sustainability issues. Climate change brings with it the possibility of dramatic sea level rise.

2.   *Large Capital:* Implementing solutions to the problems of urbanization and achieving urban sustainability requires large amounts of capital, exceptional managerial skill, and significant alignment of interests. Many corporations and investors assume that fixing cities is the responsibility of government, but governments around the world are stuck—financially, politically, or both.

3.   *Water Scarcity:* Water is an important raw material in construction and the sector must ensure efficiency in its water usage. Acute water shortage, especially in the developing world, is a major concern. The construction sector can be a part of the solution for water scarcity by developing new water infrastructure. Additional investment needed for developing water infrastructure should be provided. By working with investors and policymakers, the construction sector can help accelerate these necessary developments and help protect the water supplies of the world's most vulnerable communities.

4.   *Urbanization:* The size of global urban population has increased exponentially since the advent of the industrial revolution, with urban centers attracting large numbers of workers and families looking for opportunities for employment, education, and better quality of life. Urban populations have on average been healthier and more affluent compared to their rural counterparts. Urbanization and economic restructuring have impacted urban settlements and their people in a variety of ways. Urban labor markets shift to a growth in the service sector and a decline in the manufacturing business. Less investments and less money for education and health will be the inevitable result. The rapid growth of urban slums and squatter settlements is one of the most visible signs. These areas are the ones that are most threatened by the effects of climate changes and where most of the economically vulnerable people live. All this will lead to increasing poverty and inequality.

5. *Urban Health Equity:* Climate change, pollution, inadequate housing, and unsustainable production and consumption are threatening environmental justice and health equity among urban dwellers. Vulnerable groups (young children, the elderly, the poor, and those with compromised health) are likely to suffer more from environmental pollution and climate extremes, such as heatwaves, floods and droughts. More gender and age-sensitive strategies can help address inequities in urban health.

3.9 CONCLUSION

Cities are regarded as the engine of economic growth. They play a critical role for sustainable development. The concept of sustainable city is a relatively recent and has gained attention in the international community. However, the impacts of human activities in cities are increasing and causing great deal of environmental, social, and economic challenges both at local and global levels.

Sustainable cities have been the leading paradigm of urbanism. To be truly sustainable, a city must be sustainable in all areas. Some cities seem to take the notion of sustainability more seriously than others [31]. For more information about general intelligence, one should consult the books in [32-52] and the following related journals:

- *Sustainability*

- *Sustainable Cities and Society*

- *Sustainable Development*

- *Frontiers in Sustainable Cities*

- *International Journal of Urban Sustainable Development*

REFERENCE

[1]1"Sustainable cities,"

https://www.unenvironment.org/regions/asia-and-pacific/regional-initiatives/supporting-resource-efficiency/sustainable-cities

[2]	A. Sodiq et al., "Towards modern sustainable cities: Review of sustainability principles and trends," Journal of Cleaner Production, vol. 227, no. 1, August 2019, pp. 972-1001.

[3]	M. N. O. Sadiku, U. C. Chukwu, A. Ajayi-Majebi, and S. M. Musa, "Sustainable cities," International Journal of Trend in Scientific Research and Development, vol. 5, no. 6, September-October 2021, pp. 731-738.

[4]	"Indicators for sustainable cities," November 2015,

https://ec.europa.eu/environment/integration/research/newsalert/pdf/indicators_for_sustainable_cities_IR12_en.pdf

[5]	"Sustainable living,"

https://www.bbc.co.uk/bitesize/guides/zqvxdmn/revision/1

[6]	M. Höjer and J. Wangel, "Smart sustainable cities definition and challenges,"

https://www.researchgate.net/publication/265594929_Smart_Sustainable_Cities_Definition_and_Challenges

[7]	M. N. O. Sadiku, O. D. Olaleye, and S. M. Musa, "Green cities: A tutorial," International Journal of Trend in Research and Development, vol. 6, no. 3, May- Jun. 2019, pp. 77-79.

[8]	R. Ruhil, "Millennium Development Goals to Sustainable Development Goals: Challenges in the health sector," International Studies, vol. 52, no. 1–4, 2017, pp. 118–135.

[9]	"17 Companies helping meet the 17 UN Sustainable Development Goals,"

https://fi.co/insight/17-companies-helping-meet-the-17-un-sustainable-development-goals

[10] World Health Organization, "From MDGs to SDGs: General introduction,"

https://www.who.int/gho/publications/mdgs-sdgs/MDGs-SDGs2015_chapter1.pdf?ua=1

[11]   "Sustainable city," Wikipedia, the free encyclopedia https://en.wikipedia.org/wiki/Sustainable_city

[12]   "Top 10: Sustainable cities around the world,"

https://www.lux-review.com/top-10-sustainable-cities-around-the-world/

[13]   "Why the world needs a fresh take on smart and sustainable infrastructure," November 2021,

https://www.weforum.org/agenda/2021/11/smart-sustainable-infrastructure/

[14]   "Sustainable infrastructure, a must in the fight against climate change,"

https://www.iberdrola.com/sustainability/sustainable-infrastructure

[15]   S. Jones, "Sustainable construction: Why building for a better world is better for business," September 2021,

https://www.autodesk.com/design-make/articles/sustainable-construction

[16]   "Sustainable transport," Wikipedia, the free encyclopedia, https://en.wikipedia.org/wiki/Sustainable_transport

[17]   M. N. O. Sadiku, Emerging Green Technologies. Boca Raton, FL: CRC Press, 2020, pp. 4,24.

[18]   "Green is the way to go for housing in VN," June 2017,

https://vietnamnews.vn/economy/377607/green-is-the-way-to-go-for-housing-in-vn.html

[19]   S. Meyer, "What is a sustainable city? 10 characteristics of green urban planning," September 2023,

https://www.thezebra.com/resources/home/what-is-a-sustainable-city/

[20]   "6 Traits of a sustainable city (with examples),"

https://www.digi.com/blog/post/sustainable-city#:~:text=6%20
Characteristics%20and%20Key%20Features%20of%20a%20
Sustainable,Farming%20...%206%206.%20Implement%20
Green%20Architecture%20

[21]   "Five sustainable cities making a difference for the planet,"
March 2017,

https://climaterealityproject.org/blog/five-sustainable-cities-making-
difference-planet

[22]   B. E. Sawe, "The world's most sustainable cities," January
2019,

https://www.worldatlas.com/articles/the-world-s-most-sustainable-
cities.html

[23]   "Sustainable cities revisited," Environment and Urbanization,
vol. 10, no. 2, October 1998, pp.3-8.

[24]   "What are the principles of urban sustainability,"

https://www.re-thinkingthefuture.com/sustainable-architecture/
a4249-what-are-the-principles-of-urban-sustainability/

[25] "Smart city: Energy challenges facing sustainable cities,"

https://www.ifpenergiesnouvelles.com/article/smart-city-energy-
challenges-facing-sustainable-cities

[26]   M.N. O. Sadiku, Emerging Green Technologies. Boca Raton,
FL: CRC Press, 2020, p. xi.

[27]   "Sustainability in the city,"

https://discountdumpsterco.com/blog/sustainability-in-the-city/

[28]   "3 areas sustainable construction can help build a greener
future," May 2022, https://www.weforum.org/agenda/2022/05/3-
ways-sustainable-construction-can-forge-a-greener-future/

[29]   "The challenge of the sustainable city,"

https://link.springer.com/article/10.1007/s10668-010-9259-3

[30]   S. Vardoulakis and P. Kinney, "Grand challenges in sustainable cities and health," Frontiers in Sustainable Cities, vol. 1, 2009,

https://www.frontiersin.org/articles/10.3389/frsc.2019.00007/full

[31]   K. E. Portney, "Taking sustainable cities seriously: A comparative analysis of twenty-four US cities," Local Environment, vol. 7, no. 4, 2002, pp. 363-380.

[32]   G. McGranahan et al. (eds.), The Citizens at Risk; From Urban Sanitation to Sustainable Cities. Earthscan Publications, 2001.

[33]   M. Jenks, M. Jenks, and N. Dempsey, Future Forms and Design for Sustainable Cities. Elsevier, 2005.

[34]   R. Zetter and G. B. Watson (eds.), Designing Sustainable Cities In The Developing World. Ashgate Publishing, 2006.

[35]   W Yang (ed.), Sustainable Cities, Development and Environment; Proceedings. Trans Tech Publications, 2012.

[36]   M. Janssens et al. (eds.), Sustainable Cities; Diversity, Economic Growth and Social Cohesion. Edward Elgar Publishing, 2009.

[37]   M. Hodson and S. Marvin (eds.), After Sustainable Cities?Abingdon, Oxford: Routledge, 2014.

[38]   L. J. Pearson, P. W. Newton, and P. Roberts, Resilient Sustainable Cities: A Future. Abingdon, Oxon: Routledge, 2014.

[39]   K. Chapple, Planning Sustainable Cities and Regions: Towards More Equitable Development. New York: Routledge. 2014.

[40]   H. Tamagawa (ed.), Sustainable Cities; Japanese Perspectives on Physical and Social Structures. United Nations University Press, 2006.

[41]   A. Grubler and D. Fisk (eds.), Energising Sustainable Cities. Abingdon, Earthscan/ Routledge, 2013.

[42]   B. Evans et al., Governing Sustainable Cities. London, Earthscan 2003.

[43]   K. E. Portney, Taking Sustainable Cities Seriously: Economic Development, The Environment, and Quality of Life in American Cities. Cambridge, MA: MIT Press, 2013.

[44]   R .White and J. Whitney, Sustainable Cities: Urbanization and the Environment In International Perspective. Avalon Publishing, 1992

[45]   R. Capello, P. Nijkamp, and G. Pepping, sustainable Cities and Energy Policies. Springer, 2012.

[46]   C. Pugh, Sustainable Cities in Developing Countries. London: Earthscan 2013.

[47]   R. Cooper, G. Evans, and C. Boyko, Designing Sustainable Cities. Wiley-Blackwell, 2009.

[48]   J. Flint and M. Raco (eds.), The Future of Sustainable Cities: Critical Reflections. Bristol: The Policy Press, 2012.

[49]   C. Pugh (ed.), Sustainable Cities in Developing Countries. Earthscan, 2013.

[50]   P. Hall, Sustainable Cities Or Town Cramming. Great Britain: Town and Country Planning Association, 1999.

[52]   S. E. Shmelev, Sustainable Cities Reimagined: Multidimensional Assessment and Smart Solutions. Routledge, 2000.

CHAPTER 4
SUSTAINABLE ENGINEERING

"The urgency of the climate crisis and the extinction that we're facing is so urgent that we felt like everybody's mission, every business' mission should be to save our home planet... We're facing this extinction crisis, and we can't turn away from it. We need the rest of business to turn toward solutions and innovations and the things that will help us survive."

– Rose Marcario

4.1 INTRODUCTION

Sustainability has been a keyword in the 21th century because it is one of the global grand challenges. For example, we hear about sustainable engineering, sustainable development, sustainable energy, sustainable software, sustainable design, sustainable living, economic sustainability, social sustainability, ecological sustainability, etc. In this same way, there has been considerable discussion about green chemistry, green engineering, green business, green manufacturing, green food, green economy, green energy, etc. The two terms (sustainability and green) are often used interchangeably. They are related as shown in Figure 4.1 [1].

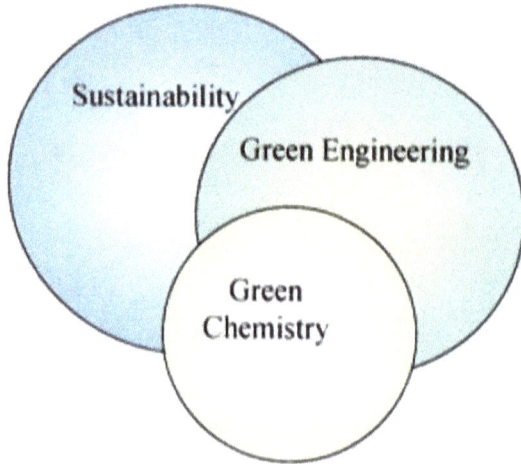

Figure 4.1 Relationship between green chemistry, green engineering, and sustainability [1].

Sustainable development has been a major driving initiative in engineering businesses throughout the world. Green engineering involves creating healthy living environments that use natural resources wisely and conservatively [2].

Engineering is the application of scientific and mathematical principles for practical purposes such as the design and operation of products and processes. It expediently utilizes resources to drive the world's economic activity, in virtually all economic sectors, e.g., military, industry, transportation, residential, commercial, agriculture, education, telecommunication, etc. Sustainable engineering (SE) is the process of designing products and systems such that they use energy and resources sustainably. It transforms existing engineering disciplines, processes, and practices to those that promote sustainability. All engineering disciplines should incorporate sustainability principles into their practice in order to improve the quality of life.

Sustainable engineering is the process of using natural resources without compromising the environment or depleting the materials for future generations. It is an important field that is concerned with finding ways to reduce the negative impact of human activity on the environment. It implies living well within the ecological limits of a finite planet. It involves the integration of social, environmental, and economic considerations into the design of product, process, and energy systems [3].

This chapter provides a brief introduction to the field of sustainable engineering. It begins with explaining the concept of sustainable engineering. It provides some applications of sustainable engineering. It highlights the benefits and challenges of sustainable engineering. The last section concludes with comments.

4.2 CONCEPT OF SUSTAINABLE ENGINEERING

Sustainable engineering may be regarded as engineering for human development that meets the needs of the present without compromising the ability of future generations to meet their own needs. Unlike traditional engineering approaches, sustainable engineering focuses on projects that are resource efficient, produce minimal pollution, and cause little to no damage to the natural environment. Sustainable engineering requires an interdisciplinary approach in all aspects of engineering and it should not be designated as a sole responsibility of environmental engineering. Sustainable engineers work to design systems and products that minimize pollution and conserve resources. Sustainable engineering typically focuses on the following areas [4]: food production, water supply, housing and shelter, sanitation and waste management, energy conservation, transportation, industrial processing, environment, pollution prevention, materials management; medical care, and appropriate use of technology.

The four pillars of sustainability analysis are energy, efficiency, environment, and society. Sustainability analysis is multi-disciplinary in nature. It requires approaches from different disciplines such as optimization, social science, and finance. Sustainability starts with green manufacturing and extends to industrial networks and then to the ecosystem. Sustainability of a system is its ability to survive and retain its functionality over time. A sustainable society is capable of surviving and prospering indefinitely.

The principles of sustainable engineering provide a paradigm in which engineers can design products and services to meet societal needs with minimal impact on the environment. Sustainable engineering should be based on principles that support sustainable development and should be applied early in design. The design must consider short and long-term impacts. It will be hard and expensive to turn back and redesign things. Sustainable engineering will provide ways to reduce a product's environmental effects at every stage of its lifecycle, from conception, development, and prototyping to commercialization, recycling, and disposal.

Today sustainability is seen in three-dimensions: environmental, economic, and socio-cultural, which are illustrated in Figure 4.2 and explained as follows [5].

Figure 4.2 Sustainability in the interaction of environment, social actions, and economics [5].

• Environmental Sustainability: The earth resources and processes are connected with human societies. Environmental sustainability describes a possible way that human societies can sustainably develop by living within the system earth and using the resources of planet earth. It is focused on three protection goals: protection of resources, the ecosystem, and human health.

• Economic Sustainability: This addresses effective investments, finance, job creation, and competitiveness.

• Social Sustainability: This addresses equity, justice, security, employment, and participation.

4.3 APPLICATIONS

Sustainable engineering is a practical challenge to all engineering disciplines The following applications are practical demonstrations of sustainable engineering.

• *Sustainable Software:* Software usage has multiple direct effects. The objective of sustainable software engineering is the enhancement of software engineering which targets the direct and indirect consumption of natural resources and energy which are caused by software systems during their entire life cycle. To achieve this requires that we start off with a "cradle to grave" perspective and develop a life cycle of software products [6].

• *Sustainable Construction:* The construction industry has its footprints on all human efforts to control, modify, and dominate nature and natural systems. There is a growing consensus that delivering a sustainable built environment starts with incorporating sustainability thoughts at the planning and design stages of an infrastructure construction project. Geotechnical engineering can significantly influence the sustainability of infrastructure development because of its early position in the construction process [7]. Sustainable construction is regarded as the construction of a building having minimal impact on the environment. It is the practice of creating a healthy environment that is based on ecological principles. It focuses on six principles: conserve, reuse, recycle/renew, protect nature, create nontoxic, and high quality. The goal of sustainable construction is to reduce the industry's impact on the environment by utilizing sustainable development practices. Certain construction practices, methods, and materials are proven to be more earth-friendly and enhance sustainable efforts. Construction projects that develop green buildings (homes, hospitals, office, factory, etc.) benefit both the environment and the people inside them [8]. Figure 4.3 shows different components of sustainable construction [9], while Figure 4.4 illustrates a typical example of sustainable construction [10].

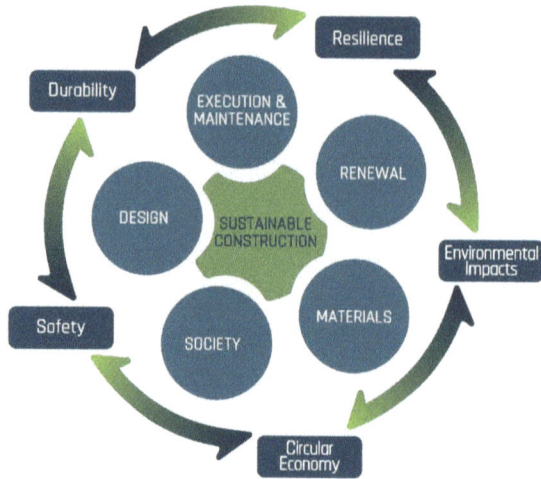

Figure 4.3 Different components of sustainable construction [9].

Figure 4.4 A typical example of sustainable construction [10].

• *Sustainable Materials:* One way to practice sustainability in construction is through the building materials (metals, plastics, paper, cardboard, etc.) that are used. Materials, as a key resource, renewable or non-renewable have far reaching consequences for the sustainability of our society through their fundamental role in meeting the needs of current and future generations. A new generation of stronger, lighter, and revolutionary building materials can help solve many problems in the industry as well as push current practices to be more sustainable. These materials have the added benefit of protecting the environment by reducing the carbon footprint of the buildings. For example, bamboo is one of the most sustainable construction materials. Construction projects can utilize bamboo in various applications like supporting concrete, scaffolding, roofing, and building other structures [8].

• *Civil Engineering:* Sustainability can be incorporated into civil engineering projects in many ways, including designing for efficiency, minimizing environmental impacts, considering the project's lifecycle, and engaging the community. Sustainable engineering is a critical and evolving field that plays a vital role in developing and maintaining our built environment. Sustainable engineering projects often incorporate design elements that maximize efficiency and minimize the use of resources. This can include using locally sourced, recycled, or renewable materials and designing buildings and infrastructure to maximize energy and water efficiency. Civil engineers play an important role in building and maintaining the infrastructure that underpins our communities and economies. They engineer the structural solutions of tomorrow and plan, design, construct, and operate the infrastructure essential to our modern lives. By adopting sustainable practices, civil engineers can help to create an infrastructure that is sustainable and responsible. They can also contribute to a more sustainable future and help to address global challenges such as climate change and resource depletion. A civil engineer is shown in Figure 4.5 [11].

Figure 4.5 A civil engineer at work [11].

• *Sustainable Manufacturing:* Manufacturing is part of the supply chain between suppliers and customers of a manufacturing company. It is critical to achieve sustainability and sustainable development. Manufacturing operations create value by transforming raw materials into finished products by using energy, material, and other resources, which may cause environmental impact. Due to rapid globalization, manufacturing organizations now operate in the form of global production networks, and their value creation process spans across the globe. The core function of manufacturing is to create value through a process of material transformations. While these negative externalities impact both local and global ecosystems, logistics and outsourcing decisions of manufacturing organizations have a wide-ranging environmental impact. For manufacturing organizations to move towards sustainable practices, sustainability needs to be embedded into the planning from strategic, long term, to operational, short term planning. Several organizations have investigated how to incorporate sustainability into manufacturing organizations. To operationalize absolute sustainability, it is crucial for manufacturing organizations to have a strategic plan towards achieving the reductions in environmental impact. This requires strategic planning of product and product technologies that need to be targeted for the necessary impact reduction while maintaining viability of the business [12].

Figure 4.6 shows a sustainable manufacturing facility, where the combination of abundant daylight and natural ventilation creates acomfortable, productive workplace [13].

Figure 4.6 A sustainable manufacturing facility [13].

• *Sustainable Tissue Engineering:* Tissue engineering is associated with living cells, materials, and methods, as well as biochemical and physicochemical factors to improve or replace biological tissues. It has its origins in the late 1980s. It is the creation of new tissue for the therapeutic reconstruction of the human body. The field has been practicing a green approach for decades by fabricating sustainable biomaterials using natural sources or by-products. A number of cell-based tissue engineering products have been designed, some of which have been subject to clinical trials. Several of the early tissue-engineering biomaterials were modeled on those absorbable materials that had been used in FDA approved surgical sutures. The simple concept of a scaffold guiding a tissue regeneration process is insufficiently robust to result in effective, sustainable, tissue engineering [14].

• *Hydroponics:* The traditional methods used in the farming industry take up lot of room and consume vast amount of resources. Hydroponics is looking to change that. Hydroponics involves growing plants in a nutrient-rich solution, oftentimes without a medium like soil. Since hydroponic techniques allow for plants to be grown indoors and without direct sunlight, some hydroponic specialists are taking crops that are traditionally grown outside in the fields and moving them into towering skyscrapers. This method is known as vertical farming. By growing crops inside a building with multiple floors, the farming project takes up less land and is able to grow the crops in a controlled environment. This vertical hydroponics system also requires less water than traditional farming. Hydroponics creates a farming system that is far less taxing on the environment [15].

•   *Sustainable Engineering Education:* Higher education is now facing new challenges as it prepares future professionals. Engineers of the future will face more demanding challenges as they must design human-environment-technology systems. Engineering education is responsible for developing programs that will lead to a better, safer, and moral modern future world. Critical topics such as global warming, climate change, green practices and sustainable engineering solutions are central to recent changes to regulations and policies impacting the practice of engineering. In view of this every engineering curricula should incorporate sustainability as an overarching theme. A degree program in sustainable engineering should be useful for engineers and non-engineers alike. Such a degree program may cover basic sciences (chemistry, biology, physics), atmospheric science, social science, economics, geography and planning, and political science. It should have great potential for hands-on multidisciplinary project-based learning [16,17].

•   *Engineering Sustainable Happiness:* Everyone wants to be happy and strives to be happy. The notion of happiness is expanded to sustainable happiness. Sustainable happiness is the pursuit of happiness that does not exploit other people, the environment or future generation. By influencing decision making processes, sustainable happiness can guide individuals, communities and politicians. The key element of it is cooperation between people. Creating positive mind-sets and developing honesty and mutual trust ultimately lead towards sustainable happiness [18].

Other areas of application include sustainable hydraulic engineering, sustainable road mobility, and sustainable critical infrastructures (e.g. electric power infrastructure, transportation infrastructure, food and water infrastructures, financial infrastructure, and telecommunication infrastructures).

4.4 BENEFITS

Sustainability is important for a variety of reasons, including a better quality of life, bettering one's personal satisfaction, securing the climate, and environmental quality. It is a holistic approach that addresses environmental, social, and economic issues in infrastructure design, construction, and maintenance. It has many benefits including environmental, resource, and cost savings, enhanced quality of life, and social and economic benefits. It helps to get cleaner air in the cities, reduce waste, produce food locally, contribute to improving the standards of living, use renewable resources, conserve energy, and clean up the planet. Engineering companies are finding numerous financial benefits and higher employment rates by developing and using new forms of sustainable engineering. New residential and commercial buildings should be designed to be more environmentally friendly. This will reduce emissions, illnesses, and energy consumption. Other benefits of sustainable engineering include the following [11,19]:

1.   *Green Technology:* Green technology refers to a diverse range of technologies and practices that can be used to minimize environmental impact. It helps reduce energy and water consumption, reduces waste, reduces our carbon footprint, and improves business efficiency by lowering costs while improving product design and creating new jobs. Compared to traditional technologies, green technology reduces the impact on the environment, reduces costs, and improves our quality of life.

2.   *Reduces Energy Consumption:* Sustainable engineering helps to reduce energy consumption by pursuing energy efficiency in every aspect of the product lifecycle. Efficient machinery will reduce the energy needed for manufacturing, while sustainable product design will be applied to minimize the energy consumption of the finished product. Businesses and households can easily knock off their energy bills by simply transitioning to a green tech solution.

3.   *Reduces Water Consumption:* Water is a precious resource on our planet, and making sure to not waste it is paramount. Industrial

processes and households are using large quantities of water. Sustainable engineering helps to reduce water consumption. This can be achieved by using only what is strictly necessary for the task. The difference between a washing machine equipped with green technology and a traditional one can be huge; in fact, eco-friendly washing machines use up to 74% less water than older models. Engineers are improving the design of industrial and domestic machinery to reduce water consumption. This is not only done for the environment but also for cost reasons: a machine that uses less water, less energy, and requires less maintenance is not only more eco-friendly but also cheaper to run for the business.

4. *Reduces Air Pollution:* Traffic and polluting industries are the major contributors to air pollution in our cities. Green technologies such as hybrid and electric vehicles are increasingly been used and incentivized to reduce air pollution in the cities. Electrification of transport technologies is an important step in the right direction. There is no doubt that in the coming years, the air in our cities will become cleaner due to green technologies.

5. *Reduces Carbon Footprint:* From recycling to more rational use of natural resources, green energy is going to play a big role in helping us reduce our carbon footprint. Reducing the carbon footprint is especially challenging for energy-intensive industries like mining and manufacturing. More and more industries are voluntarily offsetting their carbon emissions by buying carbon credits, which are obtained by companies when they do something to reduce the levels of CO_2 in the atmosphere.

6. *Reduces Waste:* Recycling has the benefit of turning waste into a resource. Recovered materials are reducing the amount of solid waste reaching landfills and at the same time, they are also reducing the need to continuously extract new raw materials from our planet, helping to preserve its natural resources. Both businesses and the environment are benefiting from this because the cardboard is not ending up in the landfill and companies can also make some profit by recycling it.

7. *Cost Savings:* Sustainable engineering projects can offer cost savings over the long term due to their resource efficiency and durability. For example, a building that is energy efficient may require

less energy to operate, leading to lower energy bills, and maintenance costs.

8.   *Social Equity:* Sustainable engineering aims to promote social equity by ensuring that infrastructure projects are inclusive and responsive to the needs of all community members, regardless of their socioeconomic status. Equity and just distribution and use of the limited resources allow the transition to sustainable consumption and production to occur in parallel with a socially sustainable development for the large population groups that still today live in poverty. Societal and behavioral changes are essential for sustainable development.

9.   *Tax Incentives:* Governments are getting more and more on board to support the journey towards sustainable development. Subsidies and tax incentives to switch sustainable technologies are now very common in the United States and Europe. As a result, an additional advantage of green technology is being able to benefit from tax incentives and other grants that governments are supporting to promote the green revolution and help save the planet.

10.   *Resource Efficiency:* Sustainable engineering projects are designed to be resource efficient, which means they use fewer resources and generate less waste than traditional projects. This can help reduce the demand for raw materials and energy and lead to cost savings.

11.   *Energy Efficiency:* This can be achieved via either interaction between economically independent companies or interaction between suppliers and customers. Efficiency improvement may happen through exchanging and utilizing flows of materials and/or energy to their mutual benefit.

Some of these benefits are shown in Figure 4.7.

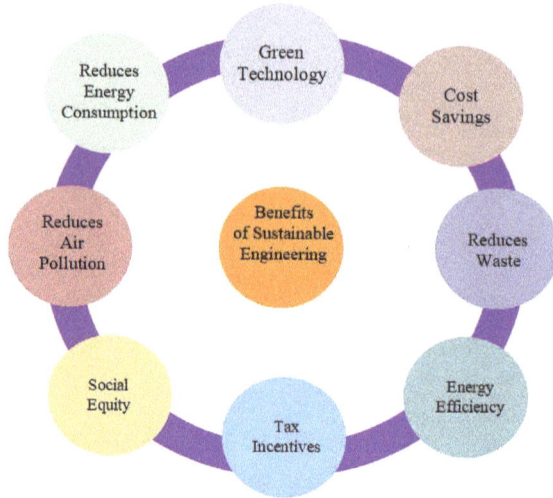

Figure 4.7 Some benefits of sustainable engineering.

4.5 CHALLENGES

Sustainable engineering poses a difficult set of challenges for engineers. Economics is one of the most prominent barrier encountered by practitioners attempting to introduce sustainable engineering practices. Designers are often expected to follow building codes and regulations which may conflict with the principles of sustainable engineering [20]. Other challenges of sustainable engineering include the following [11,21]:

1. *Wicked Problems:* Sustainable engineering problems are often regarded as wicked problems because they share the five most relevant characteristics of wicked problems [7]: (i) they are difficult to formulate,(ii) multiple but incompatible solutions exist, (iii) time frames are open-ended, (iv) the problems are unique, and (v) competing value systems or objectives exist in the problem.

2. *Climate Change:* As the effects of climate change increase, sustainability becomes even more important. Engineers are increasingly focused on designing infrastructure that is resilient to the impacts of climate change, such as sea level rise, flooding, and extreme weather events.

3. *Complexity:* Sustainable infrastructure projects can be complex

and require the integration of multiple disciplines and stakeholders. This can make coordinating and managing these projects challenging.

4.   *Switching:* Although the benefits of sustainable engineering are clear, making the switch is anything but a simple one. For example, switching to a more sustainable construction takes time and preparation to utilize the best practices. Training needs to be implemented in order to start practicing sustainable methods which takes time and money. Construction companies are not the only ones that can change their methods for the betterment of the environment. Regular people working on their own private projects can focus on utilizing sustainable engineering methods.

5.   *Cost:* Another obstacle that many companies may come across is the actual principal cost of sustainable engineering. The predominant conviction is that sustainable structure is usually more costly. Sustainable infrastructure projects can often be more expensive to design and build than traditional projects, which can be a barrier to their adoption.

6.   *Limited Resources:* Another challenge is the limited availability of resources such as funding, skilled labor, and materials. This can make it difficult to implement sustainable infrastructure projects, particularly in resource-constrained or developing areas.

7.   *Regulation:* Sustainable engineering can be impacted by various regulations and standards, varying by region and sector. Ensuring compliance with these regulations can be challenging, particularly for innovative new projects.

8.   *Public Perception:* Another challenge is the public perception of sustainable infrastructure projects. Some people may be skeptical of or resistant to these projects, making it difficult to secure support and funding.

4.6 CONCLUSION

Sustainable engineering is the process of using resources in a way that does not compromise the environment or deplete the materials for future generations.

It aims to design, build, and maintain an environmentally responsible, socially equitable, and economically viable infrastructure. It takes environmental engineering concepts to the next level by looking at the interactions between technical, ecological, social, and economic systems. There is a great deal of interest in sustainability at the moment and a more sustainable future is ahead of us. However, sustainability is a task which cannot be addressed only by individual persons or nations. It is rather an all-embracing task including aspects of each engineering discipline, which have to be addressed on a global scale. Scientists and engineers must collaborate in international and multidisciplinary groups [22].

Engineers should cultivate the habit of making our daily engineering practice as sustainable as possible. Sustainability should be embedded into all dimensions of engineering. Every engineering curricula should incorporate sustainability as an overarching theme. A degree program in sustainable engineering should be useful for engineers and non-engineers alike.

Sustainable engineering is important to building a more sustainable and resilient future. As the demand for sustainable infrastructure continues to grow, there will be increasing opportunities for engineers to contribute to this field. The prospects for sustainability engineering are bright, as there is increasing demand for more resilient, resource-efficient, and socially equitable infrastructure. More information about sustainable engineering can be found in the books in [23-38] and the journals devoted to it:

- *Sustainability*

- *Journal of Sustainable Engineering and Science*

- *Journal of Sustainability, Energy, & Environment*

- *International Journal of Sustainable Engineering*

- *International Journal of Sustainable Transportation*

- *International Journal of Global Sustainability*

- *International Journal of Sustainable Engineering Methods*

- *International Journal of Sustainable Construction Engineering & Technology*

- *International Journal of Sustainable Development Research*

- *International Journal of Sustainable Civil Engineering*

- *International Journal of Sustainable Construction Engineering & Technology*

- *International Journal of Sustainable Development*

- *International Journal of Sustainable Development and Planning*

- *International Journal of Energy and Environmental Engineering*

- *International Journal of Environmental Engineering Science and Technology Research*

REFERENCE

[1]   M. Abraham, "Sustainable engineering: An initiative for chemical engineers,"

Environmental Progress, vol.23, no.4, December 2004, pp. 261-263.

[2]   M. N. O. Sadiku, S. R. Nelatury, and S.M. Musa, "Green engineering: A primer," Journal of Scientific and Engineering Research, vol. 5, no.7, 2018, pp. 20-23.

[3]   M. N. O. Sadiku, O. D. Olaleye, and S. M. Musa, "Sustainable engineering: An introduction," International Journal of Advances in Scientific Research and Engineering, vol. 5, no. 6, June 2019, pp.70-74.

[4]   "Sustainable engineering," Wikipedia, the free encyclopedia https://en.wikipedia.org/wiki/Sustainable_engineering

[5]   Athena, "Sustainable development,"

http://macaulay.cuny.edu/eportfolios/akurry/2011/12/21/sustainable-development/

[6]   T. Johann et al., "Sustainable development, sustainable software, and sustainable software engineering: An integrated approach," Proceedings of International Symposium on Humanities, Science and Engineering Research, 2011, pp. 34-39.

[7]   D. Basu, A. Misra, and A. J. Puppala, "Sustainability and geotechnical engineering: perspectives and review," Canadian Geotechnical Journal, vol. 52, 2015, pp. 96-113.

[8]   "20 Sustainable building materials for a greener future," March 2023,

https://www.bigrentz.com/blog/sustainable-construction

[9]   "GLOBE - Global consensus on sustainability in the built environment,"

http://globe-consensus.com/

[10]   "6 Of the most amazing sustainable construction around the

world," April 2021,

https://malaysia.news.yahoo.com/6-most-amazing-sustainable-construction-221020188.html

[11]   "Transform into a green hero in just 5 minutes each day!" Unknown Source.

[12]   M. Z. Hauschild et al., "Absolute sustainability: Challenges to life cycle engineering," CIRP Annals, vol. 69, no. 2, 2020, pp. 533-553.

[13]   "Air manufacturing innovation facility expansion,"

https://www.henneberyeddy.com/project/air-manufacturing-innovation-facility/

[14]   D. F. Williams, "Challenges with the development of biomaterials for sustainable tissue engineering,"

https://www.frontiersin.org/articles/10.3389/fbioe.2019.00127/full

[15]   "3 Real sustainable engineering projects," Unknown Source.

[16]   L. A. Dempere, "Understanding sustainability through reverse engineering," IEEE Technology and Society Magazine, Fall 2010, pp.

[17]   M. D. Cristinaa, "Promoting technological entrepreneurship through sustainable engineering education," Procedia Technology, vol. 22, 2016, pp. 1129 – 1134.

[18]   N. Kobza, "Engineering sustainable happiness," IFAC-PapersOnLine, vol. 48, 2015, pp. 195–200.

[19]   "Top 10 benefits of green technology," December 2023, https://sustainability-success.com/benefits-of-green-technology/

[20]   H. Meryman and R. Silman, "Sustainable engineering – using specifications to make it happen," Structural Engineering International, vol. 14, no. 3, 2004, pp. 216-219.

[21]   D. Y. Patil, "Sustainable construction: Methods, benefits and challenges,"

https://engg.dypvp.edu.in/blogs/sustainable-construction-methods-benefits-and-challenges

[22]   G. Seliger, S. Kernbaum, and M. Zett, "Remanufacturing approaches contributing to sustainable engineering," Gestão & Produção, ol. 13, no. 3, September/December 2006, pp. 368-386.

[23]   K. Ghavami et al., Non-Conventional Materials and Technologies for Sustainable Engineering. Trans Tech Publications, 2014.

[24]   J. Perl, Sustainability Engineering: A Design Guide for the Chemical Process Industry. Springer, 2016.

[25]   G. Jonker and J. Harmsen, Engineering for Sustainability: A Practical Guide for Sustainable Design. Elsevier Science, 2012.

[26]   D. F. X. Mathaisel, J. M. Manary, and N. H. Criscimagna, Engineering for Sustainability. Taylor & Francis, 2012.

[27]   B. R. Bakshi, Sustainable Engineering: Principles and Practice. Cambridge University Press, 2019.

[28]   T. Ramjeawon, Introduction to Sustainability for Engineers. Boca Raton, FL: CRC Press, 2020.

[29]   N. A. W. A. Zawawi(ed.), Challenges for Sustainable Future: Proceedings of the 3rd International Conference on Civil, Offshore and Environmental Engineering (ICCOEE 2016, Malaysia, 15-17 Aug 2016). Boca Raton, FL: CRC Press, 2016.

[30]   B. R. Allenby, Theory and Practice of Sustainable Engineering. Pearson, 2011.

[31]   E. C. D. Tan (ed.), Sustainability Engineering Challenges, Technologies, and Applications. Boca Raton, FL: CRC Press, 2023.

[32]   K. L. Wasewar and S. N. Rao (eds.), Sustainable Engineering, Energy, and the Environment: Challenges and Opportunities. Apple Academic Press, 2022.

[33]   D. A. Vallero and C. Brasier, Sustainable Design: The Science of Sustainability and Green Engineering. Wiley, 2008.

[34]   J. Kauffman and K. Mo. Lee, Handbook of Sustainable Engineering. Springer Verlag, 2013.

[35] D. T. Allen and D. R. Shonnard, Sustainable Engineering: Concepts, Design and Case Studies. Prentice Hall, 2012.

[36] R. L. Rag and L. D. Remesh, Introduction to Sustainable Engineering. PHI Learning 2016.

[37] K. R. Reddy, C. Cameselle, and J. A. Adams, Sustainable Engineering: Drivers, Metrics, Tools, and Applications. John Wiley & Sons, 2019.

[38] P. Stansinoupolos et al., Whole System Design: An Integrated Approach to Sustainable Engineering. London, UK: Imprint Routledge, 2009.

CHAPTER 5
SUSTAINABLE BUSINESS

*"Sustainability is treating ourselves and our environment as
if we are to live on this earth forever."*

– Aaron Wood

5.1 INTRODUCTION

Our planet is not in good shape. The present situation of our
environment is deplorable. We are doing business in an unpredictable
world. It is one thing to start a business and another to excel to the
point that it is self-sustaining. Today, economies across the world
are grappling with unprecedented challenges traversing social,
economic and environmental dimensions of sustainability including
climate change, natural disasters, loss of biodiversity, hunger and
malnourishment, economic inequity, social insecurity, dwindling
natural resources, ever-increasing demands on our energy and food
supply, etc. [1]. These challenges are disrupting business operations
and supply chains in unexpected ways. The issue of sustainability
and specifically sustainable business is of increasing interest and
importance to businesses, sciences, government, public policy,
planning, and other fields. Climate change is a growing concern to
a company's stakeholders: your customers, partners, shareholders,
suppliers, employees and the community around you.

The impact of business on the environment and society can never
be under-estimated. Businesses are experiencing both pressure and
opportunity to establish sustainability goals if they have not already.
Taking care of the society and the environment should be the top
priority of every business. All the top forward-looking businesses,
like Nike, Adidas, Nestle, IBM, etc. are tilted towards sustainable
business. When companies fail to assume responsibility and adopt a
sustainable approach, the opposite can happen, leading to issues such

as social injustice, environmental degradation, and inequality.

Businesses use huge amounts of our planet's resources, and they in turn have huge impacts. Today's businesses, large and small, are faced with numerous issues that challenge them to respond to the concerns of their stakeholders to act in a socially responsible manner.

Sustainability in business refers to a company's strategy and actions to eliminate the adverse environmental and social impacts caused by business operations. A sustainable business (or green business) is one that ensures no harm to the environment and society. It is a company that will sustain itself in the market for a good time. A sustainable business is ideal for a modern-day environment because it has a positive impact on society and the environment. It is our joint responsibility to save the mother Earth to ensure a future for us and the next generation. Sustainable business is the requirement of the modern era. Failing to adopt a sustainable approach implies loss [2].

This chapter is a brief introduction to sustainable business. It begins with explaining the concept of sustainability. It discusses what sustainable business is all about. It addresses the principles of sustainable business and how to make business sustainable. It provides sustainable business models and some applications of sustainable business. It highlights the benefits and challenges of sustainable business. The last section concludes with comments.

5.2 CONCEPT OF SUSTAINABILITY

Sustainability, in one form or another, has been a concern for economists for well over 200 years. The concept of sustainability was originally coined in forestry, where it means never harvesting more than what the forest yields in new growth. The term "sustainability" has become popular in policy-oriented research as an expression of what public policies ought to achieve. The principal inspiration came from the Brundtland Report of 1987. Since then the concept has shifted in meaning [3].

The "Three Pillars of Sustainability" describes what sustainable development is all about. This tool conveys that sustainability consists of environmental, social, and economic factors that are vital when discussing the topic. The pillars (or dimensions) are explained as follows [4-6]:

• *Environmental Sustainability* symbolizes the importance of things like natural resources and biodiversity to support life on Earth. This seems to be the most obvious pillar. Environmental sustainability is about the natural environment and how it remains productive and resilient to support human life.

• *Social Sustainability* places importance on social structures, well-being, and harmony; all factors that poverty, wars, and injustices can affect. It encompasses notions of equity, empowerment, accessibility, participation, cultural identity, and institutional stability. This is the ability of a society to uphold universal human rights and meet people's basic needs, such as healthcare, education, and transportation.

• *Economic Sustainability* implies a system of production that satisfies present consumption levels without compromising future needs. Economics is the study of the allocation of limited resources across unlimited wants. Economies consist of markets where transactions occur.

Sustainability creates and maintains the conditions under which humans and nature can exist in productive harmony, that permit fulfilling the social, economic, and other requirements of present and future generations. There is no hard and fast rule towards sustainability; it is a long-term process. Businesses that use sustainable practices consider environmental sustainability and social and economic factors when establishing business decisions and operations. These policies are often described as green because they focus on limiting the impact of development on the environment. An organization's sustainability practices are usually analyzed against environmental, social, and governance (ESG) metrics.

5.3 WHAT IS SUSTAINABLE BUSINESS?

Traditional business was focusing only on economic growth and profit. It did not include social and environmental sustainability. The key aim of conventional business strategy is the production of economic value – generally profits – for the short to medium term. A sustainable business (or green business) is a business that strives towards a net zero carbon footprint. Sustainability in business refers to the effect companies have on the environment or society. It refers to living productively toward a healthy environment for current generations and the ones to come. Sustainability business strategy is the integration of economic, environmental, and social aims into a firm's goals, activities and planning, with the aim of creating long-term value for the firm, its stakeholders, and wider society.

Sustainable business implies balancing social, economic, and environmental considerations in business decision-making; stewarding the natural resource base upon which the business depends; giving back to the communities in which business is done; and promoting long-term value-creation for the company's investors. The National Environmental Policy Act of 1969 was enacted int the US to "create and maintain conditions under which humans and nature can exist in productive harmony, that permit fulfilling the social, economic and other requirements of present and future generations." Sustainable businesses reduce waste while providing value for customers by using renewable resources (like solar power), recycling materials or composting food waste instead of throwing it away altogether.

A sustainable business is any organization that participates in environmentally friendly or green activities to ensure that all processes, products, and manufacturing activities adequately address current environmental concerns while maintaining a profit. In general, a business is described as green or sustainable if it satisfies the following four criteria [7]:

1. It incorporates principles of sustainability into each of its business decisions.

2. It supplies environmentally friendly products or services that replace demand for nongreen products and/or services.

3. It is greener than traditional competition.

4. It has made an enduring commitment to environmental principles in its business operations.

Sustainable business practices can be internal or external. Internal efforts might include beginning an in-office recycling program, reducing energy use at an office or factory, or switching to natural gas or electric fleet vehicles. External sustainability efforts might include switching materials used to create products to those that cause less damage to the environment. Figure 5.1 describes separate financial, social and environmental "bottom lines" of companies [8]. These bottom lines are People, Planet, and Profit. Companies should apply three bottom lines instead of focusing purely on its finance.

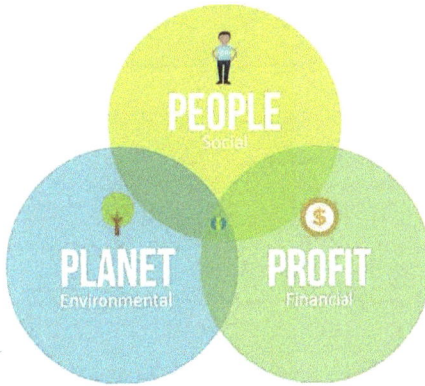

Figure 5.1 The three pillars or triple bottom lines of a sustainable business [8].

There are 3 levels of sustainability in business [9]:

• *Business Sustainability 1.0:* This is also known as refined shareholder value management and it is when environmental and social sustainability are just considered as means to a specific end.

• *Business Sustainability 2.0:* At this stage, the business is aiming at improving and balancing a triple bottom line of sustainability: economic, social, and environmental.

• *Business Sustainability 3.0:* This involves changing completely the way a business looks at the issues. At this level, the business leaders will be examining the world's problems and then looking at opportunities for how they can eventually develop solutions to improve sustainability! Not many companies are at this stage yet.

Examples of sustainability in business include [10]:

1. Utilizing sustainable materials during manufacturing.

2. Reducing greenhouse gas emissions by optimizing supply chains (factories and transportation).

3. Transitioning to renewable energy sources (solar and wind) to power facilities.

4. Giving back to local communities by sponsoring education.

5. Creating a carbon accounting system to monitor and improve the footprint.

6. Designing infrastructures that reduce emissions, preserve water and eliminate waste.

7. Promoting sustainable consumption.

8. Protecting natural resources.

9. Empowering a circular economy.

10. Exceeding expectations of external regulations.

5.4 PRINCIPLES OF SUSTAINABLE BUSINESS

The five principles of a sustainable business are [11]:

1. Anticipate change in your industry and niche, so you can figure out how to welcome those challenges without hampering the growth of your business.

2. You should know everything about your business, be it the purpose, motivation, core strengths, and everything about your customers, clients, and competitors.

3. To run a sustainable business, you should share what you know. Sharing is caring, and it paves the path of a loyal fan base.

4. Figure out how to concentrate on the different opportunities that come your way. You should approach every day with positive thinking.

5. Finally, to run a sustainable business, you should own your success and work daily with the same amount of dedication, perseverance, and accountability.

The top five most sustainable businesses of 2022 are Intel, Clorox, Ecolab, Best Buy, and PVH. For example, Starbucks with nearly 36,000 locations across the globe is heavily reliant on farmers. Their coffee farmers across the globe are struggling to adapt to global warming. Figure 5.2 shows a farmer supporting sustainable coffee farming [12].

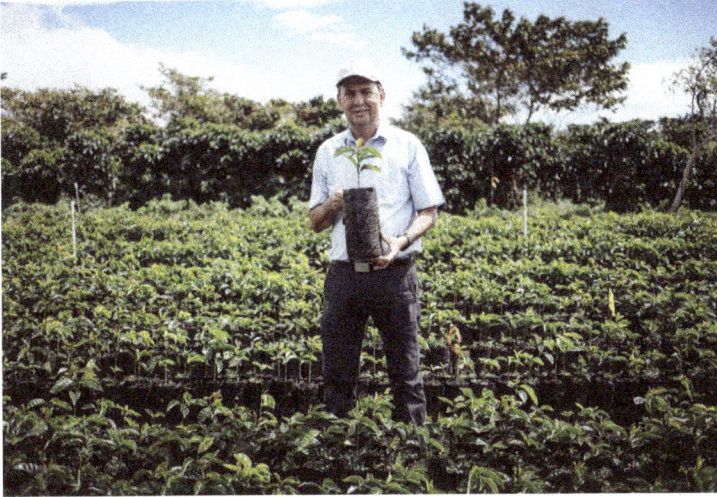

Figure 5.2 A farmer supporting sustainable coffee farming [12].

Another example of a sustainable company is Seventh Generation, which has focused on being eco-friendly since being founded in 1988. Seventh Generation's mission is "to transform the world into a healthy, sustainable & equitable place for the next seven generations." Some of their products are shown in Figure 5.3 [13].

Figure 5.3 Eco-friendly products of Seventh Generation [13].

5.5 HOW TO MAKE BUSINESS SUSTAINABLE

Corporations and businesses can be sustainable by implementing sustainable business practices, which allow a company to create a positive impact on people, society, and the environment while also making a profit. Sustainable business practices balance the three pillars of sustainability and are a way to run a business in a way that is environmentally friendly and socially responsible. Today, sustainable practices are more reachable than ever. A sustainable business can support itself and offer a profit to its owners and shareholders. Unsustainable businesses tend to be a drain on resources, and their owners shut them down after they fail to prove viable. Understanding how to create sustainable business will not only help you impress customers, but it can also help you attract committed employees who are looking to work for socially responsible businesses. To build a sustainable business involves taking the following steps [14]:

1.   *Understand What Customers Need:* Make it a top duty and priority to understand the changing needs of your customers.

2.   *Innovate To Meet Customer Needs:* One key to sustainable business is continually innovating to meet the evolving nature of consumer needs.

3. *Prioritize Your People:* Prioritizing people and giving them a clear purpose for their work is a recipe for success and sustainable business.

4. *Have Well-Defined Processes:* Having clear-cut and defined processes can help teammates understand how to quickly approach day-to-day business operations to achieve success without constant oversight.

5. *Be Authentic:* Always be authentically you in your dealings with your consumers, buyers, and business associates.

6. *Never Get Complacent:* Complacency may find its way into the culture of the company and must be resisted.

7. *Lead With Integrity:* Building a sustainable business is always about integrity. A lot of companies crumble because their business was built on rocky ground.

8. *Focus on Communication and Culture:* Especially in times of crisis, the quality of communication is central to how employees will evaluate culture and contribute to the overall longevity and sustainability of a business.

9. *Be A Flexible Employer:* If you want to get the most out of your team, help them fit work around their other priorities.

10. *Create Brand Loyalty:* Brand loyalty is one of the critical elements that can help sustain your business even during an economic crisis.

11. *Promote Carpooling:* To encourage employees to reduce fuel consumption, companies can implement telecommuting and carpooling policies. An example of an employee who rides bike to work is shown in Figure 5.4 [16].

Figure 5.4 An employee who rides bike to work [16].

5.6 SUSTAINABLE BUSINESS MODELS

In essence, business models describe the way business is done. There are many manifestations and depictions of business models: focusing on activities, values, providing a conceptual template of a business or providing a process-oriented perspective. Sustainable business models (SBMs) have become of interest because of rising sustainability concerns coupled with concerns for competitiveness. They allow for a holistic view on how business is done.

Sustainability falls under the umbrella of corporate social responsibility corporate social responsibility (CSR), which is a sustainable business practice where companies are developing programs that help the surrounding communities and society at large. CSR includes things such as:

• *Promoting Equality and Inclusivity:* keeping a diverse workforce and supporting minorities in the business.

• *Corporate Citizenship:* The idea of corporate citizenship is to create a company culture where employees feel empowered to make positive changes in their community.

• *Corporate Philanthropy:* This refers to giving back financially or through volunteering time by corporations, not just employees but also shareholders as well. Corporations can give money directly or use other means such as grants or donations for specific projects like building houses for disadvantaged families in need.

• *Corporate Giving Programs:* This is a mechanism used by companies to promote goodwill among customers and employees while helping the community at large.

An eco-friendly business, or "green business" is one that demonstrates a commitment to an environmentally sustainable future. It is an operation that unionizes concern for the environment, profitability, and goodwill for the common good as its forefront. A sustainable business model helps generate value for everyone involved, without draining the resources that help to create it. A sustainable business model is what every business leader hopes to achieve — a business that will turn a profit quickly. A truly sustainable business model is one that gives as much as it takes There are four key elements of a sustainable business model [15]:

1. A sustainable business model is commercially profitable.

2. A sustainable business model can succeed far into the future.

3. A sustainable business model uses resources it can utilize for the long term.

4. A sustainable business model gives back.

To create a sustainable business model, consider the following tips:

• Plan your resource usage.

• Engage your customers way to show that you value your customers.

• Focus on your value proposition when you are starting a business.

• Going paperless is a simple practice to cut down on unnecessary waste.

• Focus on constant reinvention.

• Partner with employees through training.

- Find a way to give back.

5.7 APPLICATIONS OF SUSTAINABLE BUSINESS

Sustainability is an essential part of corporate responsibility today and it is a necessary step toward preserving our planet for future generations. Companies must embed sustainability into the fabric of their business to get the insights they need to operationalize at scale. Sustainable business is applied in the following areas [16]:

- *Sustainable Entrepreneurship:* Early leaders in enterprise sustainability are applying digital technologies such as AI, IoT data, blockchain and hybrid cloud to help operationalize sustainability at scale. Sustainable entrepreneurship is a continuous dynamic process of change that is pushed by new ideas and creative approaches towards social and economic solutions. Promotion of the idea of entrepreneurship is beneficial for unemployed people, and the greatest beneficiaries are the youths who are the handlers of the future in every society. Although there are hundreds of professions for young people, many of them freely and willingly go for entrepreneurship as their career track [17].

- *Sustainable Workplace:* A sustainable business takes care of employees and their workplace. Employees are the heart of any corporation and business. It is important to take care of them in order to create a healthy workplace and achieve social and human sustainability for the business. Building a culture where everyone feels valued and cherished is key to creating an environment where people enjoy going to work daily. A great place to start when it comes to incorporating a sustainable lifestyle in the workplace is to provide each employee with some branded, reusable products. This will drastically reduce your waste. A sustainable workplace is committed to using sustainable stationary and notebooks, typically shown in Figure 5.5 [18]. Providing reusable utensils, bowls, plates, etc. in the kitchen area of your office is another great way to discourage wasteful behavior.

Figure 5.5 A sustainable workplace uses sustainable stationary and notebooks [18].

• *Sustainable Workforce:* Employees are looking for more than just a place to work. They are increasingly looking for mission-driven, purpose-led employers who care about the planet when deciding where to work. The workforce is now driven by generations that care about their company's social and environmental impact. The workforce has shifted its priorities as the world's practices have progressed. Digital natives care about three factors when searching for their ideal company: ethics, environment, and wellbeing and inclusion. A job is more fulfilling for employees when they can make a positive social or environmental impact. Employees have stronger loyalty for a company that facilitates opportunities to create a positive impact. A typical sustainable workforce is shown in Figure 5.6 [19].

Figure 5.6 A typical sustainable workforce [19].

• *Sustainable Supply Chain Management:* The sequence of activities that allows a company to deliver its products or services to the end consumer is the supply chain. Consumers are becoming more concerned about the traceability of the goods they purchase, and supply chain leaders are looking to invest in circular economies that encourage reuse. Blockchain solutions can provide greater supply chain visibility with up-to-the minute inventory views and performance insights that help build trust and transparency. Sustainable supply chain management is a practice that aims to minimize the environmental impact of products and services from their inception through consumption.

• *Sustainable Marketing:* This is also known as green marketing. It is regarded as creating and maintaining sustainable relationships not only with customers but also with the natural and social environment. It is important to use advertisements that consider preservation and care for nature to ensure that your sustainable business exists and lives according to your values. This shows your commitment and passion for sustainability even in advertising practices. Sustainable companies should develop effective green marketing strategies and products with honesty and genuine commitment to sustainability to earn the loyalty and respect of consumers. Sustainable marketing is illustrated in Figure 5.7[20].

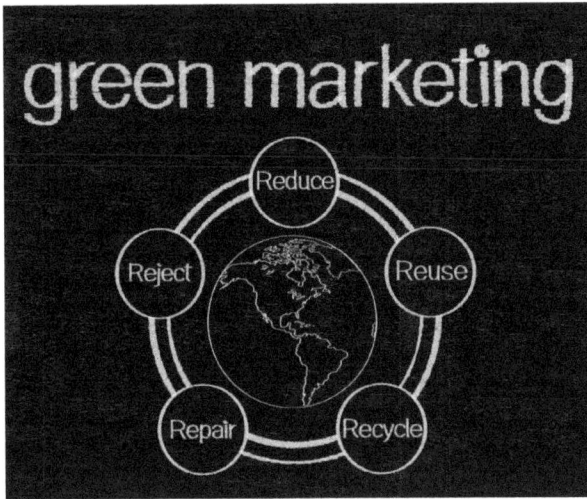

Figure 5.7 Sustainable marketing [20].

Sustainable Tourism: It is widely understood that sustainability is key to minimize the negative impacts of tourism and maximize the positive impacts. Embedding sustainable practices into all aspects of a tourism business has become more common today. Tourism is well-placed to help meet local, national, and global sustainability commitments with the implementation of sustainable actions across all operations [21].

Other areas of application of sustainable business include sustainability leadership, sustainable investing, sustainable manufacturing, sustainable transportation, urban agriculture, renewable energy, self-driving electric cars, etc.

5.8 BENEFITS

Incorporating sustainability into a business strategy is no longer a debate but widely accepted. Sustainability is a positive thing that comes with numerous benefits to the organization. A sustainable business is one that takes a holistic approach. Sustainability-focused businesses strengthen economic development and society, which are dependent on a healthy planet. They help to create a brand image and mitigate risk. No business operates in isolation; it exists within an ecosystem. The obvious benefit of operating a sustainable business is protecting the environment. Besides helping curb global challenges, sustainability can drive business success. The overlap between social and environmental progress and financial gain is called the shared value opportunity, as shown in Figure 5.8 [22].

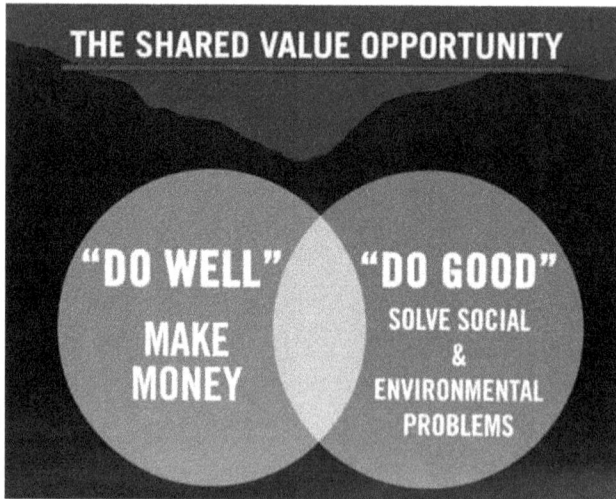

Figure 5.8 Shared value opportunity [22].

This implies that "doing good" can have a direct impact on your company's ability to "do well." Besides the feel-good impact that comes with making the world a better place, environmentally conscious and sustainable businesses cater to a rapidly growing market. Sustainability is crucial to longevity in a business. Other benefits include [9,10,23,24]:

• *Cost Reduction:* Waste disposal, water and energy consumption, and material use cost money. This directly affects profit. So, if a business efficiently manages their use of these items, costs will drop, which means an increase in profit.

• *Attract Customers:* Customers have learned to use their money wisely. They wield it for the causes they care about, and the public cares more about the environment every day. Sustainable business practices lower costs, create more competitive advantages, foster opportunities for growth, reduce risks, and create the potential for more profit.

• *Competitive Advantage:* Customers want to do their part in positively impacting the environment and are increasingly choosing businesses that care about the environment and practice sustainability. It is appropriate to be open about your sustainability goals and use your sustainability as a selling point. Being known as a sustainable business can improve your brand awareness and help you attract consumers. Make sure to present your brand so that it is irresistible to potential customers and buyers.

• *Investor Appeal:* Like consumers, investors are turning their attention toward business sustainability. Today investors are keeping the sustainability factors in mind while investing. Investors examine factors such as a company's carbon footprint, water usage, community development efforts, and board diversity. Sustainable business practices are critical in attracting new customers and investors and staying compliant. Sustainable development within a business can create value for customers, investors, and the environment.

• *Regulation:* When a business focuses on its sustainability and long-term success, it becomes easy for the business to comply and implement some of the government's legal requirements for the industry.

• *Compliance:* In 2015, the Paris Agreement was created by UN as an environmental pact for reducing greenhouse gas emissions to reduce the rising global temperature. The Paris Agreement is legally binding, and countries must comply with the rules. Compliance ensures your business can continue its operations.

• *Talent Acquisition:* Employees are increasingly choosing companies that care about the environment and practice sustainability. They are seeking purpose-driven employment and want to work for sustainable and socially responsible companies. Improve your chances of hiring the best employees by ensuring your business can be one people would be proud to work for. It is easy to attract vibrant and talented employees just because you have sustainable approaches to solving customers' issues

• *Revenue Growth:* By implementing sustainable practices that reduce resource consumption and optimize operational efficiencies, today's change agents become tomorrow's winners as they improve their bottom line. While taking the time and money to implement these new practices at first can be costly, the overall long-term payoff can ultimately benefit companies.

• *Waste Reduction:* Sustainability is all about keeping the planet healthy and clean. This means using less energy, water, and other resources to cut down on expenses. Businesses should aim to reduce their waste wherever possible. Sustainability practices in business can also be good for the company's bottom line. They help companies reduce costs and become more competitive by reducing waste and recycling products. An effective way for businesses to contribute towards waste reduction is to remanufacture products so that the materials used can have a longer lifespan. When businesses engage in sustainable production practices, the chances of wasting resources are reduced. A sustainable business recycles to ensure that all resources are used well.

• *Loyal Customer Base:* A company that practices sustainability can also build a more loyal customer base. When people feel like they are making a difference by purchasing products from an environmentally and socially responsible business, they are more likely to buy from that company again. Sustainability improves customer loyalty, which can lead to increased sales and profits. It builds relationships with customers and employees as well as growing the bottom line. Consumers nowadays are demanding more sustainable goods and services.

• *Social Impact:* Organizations that give back to the community, whether through employees volunteering their time or through charitable donations, are often considered socially sustainable. They must focus on their social impact as well as environmental impact to gain consumer loyalty. There is a stronger public image and reputation for companies that are perceived to be more socially and environmentally responsible.

• *Tax Incentives:* Choosing green energy sources and incorporating eco-friendly practices increases your chances of receiving many tax benefits. Tax incentives encourage entrepreneurs to go green. Business owners can take advantage of incentives for purchasing hybrid vehicles, doing renovations that reduce costs for heating, cooling, and lighting, as well as by making improvements to old HVAC and water heating systems. In some cases, a sustainable business may be able to get loans or grants from government or private organizations, or get tax credits or rebates.

• *Reputation:* You can improve your company image by showing how you are giving back to society. Small businesses that go green save money and improve their corporate reputation. Any time you add a green initiative to your workplace, you can use the event to generate positive public relations. Switching consumers notice when businesses make an effort to adopt green practices to help the environment. These efforts leave a lasting impression on customers, potential customers, and vendors. There are increased sales from consumers who are more likely to buy products from companies with good corporate sustainability programs.

• *Remote Working:* There is less need for people to be in a physical office. Remote working has become increasingly popular over the years. The reduced commute is great for the environment. It means that there are fewer vehicles on the road and time spent waiting in traffic. All of which equates to less carbon dioxide emissions into the air. With fewer people in the office, businesses can save money usually spent on stocking, lighting, and heating the workplace for employees.

Some of these benefits are displayed in Figure 5.9 [25].

Figure 5.9 Some of benefits of sustainable business [25].

5.9 CHALLENGES

Implementing sustainable business practices may have an effect on profits and a firm's financial "bottom line." There are several challenges to overcome in the pursuit of becoming a truly sustainable business. Numerous practices are cited as threats to sustainability, such as political corruption, social inequality, the arms race, and profligate government expenditures. Some challenges faced in the sustainable business practices implementation by businesses in developing countries include lack of skilled personnel, technological challenges, socio-economic challenges, organizational challenges, and lack of proper policy framework. A major challenge for a successful transition is the complexity of coordinating at multiple levels in the organization. Other challenges include [26]:

• *Customer Readiness:* While the mindset around sustainability is shifting, no business can afford to be left behind. Co-creating a sustainable future requires a deep understanding of your customers.

• *Cost:* Implementing sustainable business practices typically requires higher upfront investments. However, these costs are a small price to pay for a better future. Some organizations will need help building an investment case to show how immediate investment will result in more durable profitability over the long run.

• *Systemic Inertia:* While sustainability is an important goal, it often is not seen as more important than other key priorities that may provide benefits sooner. It comes back to reframing risks as opportunities and building the case that acting on sustainability now is necessary to achieving future sustainability in business.

• *Lack of Tools, Insights, and Expertise:* Being unprepared to develop a corporate sustainability vision, strategy, and framework is a monumental risk. Every business needs an ecosystem of innovation partners to help them reinvent the world and create a sustainable future.

• *Education:* One of the main challenges in promoting sustainable business practices is the lack of education and awareness. Practical solutions may include creating partnerships with universities and research institutions to develop new technologies and best practices that promote sustainable business.

• *Trust Issue:* The trust issue arises in the online business mostly because there is a reliability issue between the buyer and seller. It is a major barrier in the entrepreneurial process. Trust exists in different forms and can be differentiated as institution based, process based, or based on characteristics. Thus, the trust process, containing expectations or beliefs about the trustworthiness of others, is the common element in personal and collective trust.

• *Gender Issues:* Although men dominate business ownership, it is interesting to know that females are fast-growing as entrepreneurs globally. Male entrepreneurs are more likely to establish new businesses and accelerate activities than females. Female entrepreneurs encounter more challenges and problems in developing countries. There is more possibility of having female entrepreneurs and female-owned businesses in large cities than in small towns and rural areas. Female entrepreneurs are involved in diverse business activities including restaurants, beauty salons, child-care services, grocery stores, landscaping services, and insurance services.

• *Corruption:* Corruption is a harming factor in business. It is the illicit use of one's position or power for perceived personal or collective gain. Corruption undermines the importance of the activities intended to take place in a timely and speedy fashion. Illegal activities, corruptive practices, bribery, and illicit behaviors determine the involvement and the existence of corruption. Petty corruption is used by officials in the form of bribes to generate extra income to compensate for their low salary. Sometimes, money is not demanded, but expensive gifts or free trips are demanded in order to provide work done in a short time and simple way. Corruption is like grease on the wheel to accelerate the process and get work done in a timely manner.

Some of these challenges are illustrated in Figure 5.10 [17].

Figure 5.10 Some challenges of sustainable business [17].

5.10 CONCLUSION

Sustainability is a business imperative and should be core to the strategy and operations of every business. Most sustainable companies focus on their social and environmental impact more than profit. As science has progressed, the world has found new ways to maintain more sustainable practices. Going off-trend is never suggested for any type of business, and the trend today is sustainability. Only sustainable, environment-friendly approach can ensure the future of any business. Long-term sustainability is directly related, to long-term success. Everyone affects the sustainability of the marketplace and the planet one way or another.

A growing number of organizations are integrating sustainability into their business strategy. People are educating themselves about the need to adopt an environment-friendly approach to business. For more information on sustainable business, one should consult books in [27-43] and the following related journals:

- *Sustainability*

- *IIMBG Journal of Sustainable Business and Innovation*

- *Journal of Sustainable Business and Economics*

• *Journal of Management for Global Sustainability*

• *Journal of Sustainable Business and Management Solutions in Emerging Economies*

• *International Journal of Global Sustainability*

• *Sustainable Business Magazine*

REFERENCE

[1]   R. Mahajan and M. Bose, "Business sustainability: Exploring the meaning and significance," IMI Konnect , vol. 7, no. 2, 2018, pp. 8-13

[2]   M. N. O. Sadiku, P. O, Adebo, and J. O. Sadiku, "Sustainable business: An introduction," submitted to a journal.

[3]   T. Kuhlman and J. Farrington, "What is sustainability?" Sustainability, vol. 2, 2010, pp. 3436-3448.

[4]   A. Browne, "Explainer: What is sustainability and why is it important?" October 2022,

https://earth.org/what-is-sustainability/

[5]   "What is sustainability?"

https://www.mcgill.ca/sustainability/files/sustainability/what-is-sustainability.pdf

[6]   S. R. Elliot, "Sustainability: An economic perspective," Resources, Conservation and Recycling, vol. 44, no. 3, June 2005, pp. 263-277.

[7]   "Sustainable business," Wikipedia, the free encyclopedia https://en.wikipedia.org/wiki/Sustainable_business

[8]   O. Avramenko, "Contribute to a better world = Be a successful company. Sustainability in a shared-economy startup," February 2018,

https://medium.com/@Anaiska/contribute-to-a-better-world-be-a-successful-company-sustainability-in-a-shared-economy-startup-50cc72f2e37b

[9]   Simon, "Sustainable business practices (definition & 12 examples),"October 2023,

https://sustainability-success.com/sustainable-business-practices/

[10]   "What is sustainability in business?" February 2023,

https://www.entrepreneur.com/starting-a-business/what-is-sustainability-in-business/444473

[11]   H. Bhasin, " Sustainable business – Definition, process and principles," June 2020,

https://www.marketing91.com/sustainable-business/

[12]   D. Wiener-Bronner, "Coffee is in danger. Starbucks is working on solutions," October 2023,

https://finance.yahoo.com/news/starbucks-scientists-developing-climate-proof-131120173.html

[13]   "The 15 most environmentally friendly & sustainable companies (2023),"

https://growensemble.com/environmentally-friendly-companies/

[14]   "14 Key steps to building a sustainable business," February 2021,

https://www.forbes.com/sites/forbesbusinesscouncil/2021/02/22/14-key-steps-to-building-a-sustainable-business/?sh=7b47cb197752

[15]   D. Hendricks, "How to create a sustainable business model," March 2023,

https://www.business.com/articles/how-to-create-a-sustainable-business-model/

[16]   L. Peterson, "Role of business in environmental protection," March 2019,

https://smallbusiness.chron.com/role-business-environmental-protection-59370.html

[17]   M. N. Tunio et al., "How entrepreneurship sustains barriers in the entrepreneurial process—A lesson from a developing nation," Sustainability, vol. 13, no. 20, 2021.

[18]   A. Shewakaramani, "10 Sustainable business ideas & 11 practices for eco-success," May 2023,

https://logo.com/blog/sustainable-business-ideas

[19]   S. Wright, "How to create a sustainable business model," May

2023,

https://businessingmag.com/14610/strategy/sustainable-model/#:~:text=How%20to%20Create%20a%20Sustainable%20Business%20Model%201,4%20Find%20a%20Way%20to%20Give%20Back%20

[20] "Top marketing strategies for sustainable businesses," November 5, 2019

https://www.theenvironmentalblog.org/2019/11/top-marketing-strategies-for-sustainable-businesses/

[21] "Sustainability is the key to a positive future for tourism," October 2021,

https://acorntourism.co.uk/insights/blog/read/2021/10/sustainability-is-the-key-to-a-positive-future-for-tourism-b54

[22] A. Spiliakos, "What does 'sustainability' mean in business?" October 2018,

https://online.hbs.edu/blog/post/what-is-sustainability-in-business

[23] "10 Advantages of being a sustainable business,"

https://www.ismartrecruit.com/blog-advantages-sustainable-business

[24] "5 Benefits of sustainable business practices,"

https://www.jadetrack.com/5-benefits-of-sustainable-business-practices/

[25] "The sustainability challenge for corporate treasury," May 2019,

https://ctmfile.com/story/the-sustainability-challenge-for-corporate-treasury

[26] "What is sustainability in business?"

https://www.ibm.com/topics/business-sustainability

[27] H. Kopnina and J. Blewitt, Sustainable Business: Key Issues. Routledge, 2014.

[28] I. Ehnert, Sustainability and Human Resource Management

Developing Sustainable Business Organizations. Springer, 2014.

[29]   J. T. Scott, The Sustainable Business: A Practitioner's Guide to Achieving Long-Term Profitability and Competitiveness. Routledge, 2017.

[30]   M. Fischer et al., Sustainable Business: Managing the Challenges of the 21st Century. Springer 2023.

[31]   R. Gittell, M. Magnusson, and M. Merenda, The Sustainable Business Case Book. Saylor Foundation, 2012.

[32]   D. Young and M. Reeves (eds.), Sustainable Business Model Innovation. De Gruyter, 2023.

[33]   M. W. Tueth, Fundamentals of Sustainable Business: A Guide For The Next 100 Years. World Scientific Publishing Company, 2009.

[34]   J. Jacobsen, Sustainable Business and Industry: Designing and Operating for Social and Environmental Responsibility. ASQ Quality Press, 2011.

[35]   G. G. Lenssen and N. C. Smith (eds.), Managing Sustainable Business: An Executive Education Case and Textbook. Springer, 2018.

[36]   N. R. Sanders and J. D. Wood, Foundations of Sustainable Business: Theory, Function, and Strategy. Wiley, 2019.

[37]   F. Melissen, L. Moratis, and S. O. Idowu (eds.), Sustainable Business Models: Principles, Promise, and Practice. Springer, 2018.

[38]   D. L. Rainey, Sustainable Business Development: Inventing The Future Through Strategy, Innovation, And Leadership. Cambridge university press, 2010.

[39]   L. L. Berry, Discovering the Soul of Service: The Nine Drivers of Sustainable Business Success. Simon and Schuster, 1999.

[40]   D. Hall, I. Kirkpatrick, and M. Mitchell (eds.), Rural Tourism and Sustainable Business. Channel view publications, 2005.

[41]   G. Weybrecht, The Sustainable MBA: The Manager's Guide to Green Business. John Wiley & Sons, 2010.

[42]   S. Jørgensen, L. Jacob, and T. Pedersen, RESTART Sustainable Business Model Innovation. Springer Nature, 2018.

[43]   E. Callenbach, EcoManagement: The Elmwood Guide to Ecological Auditing And Sustainable Business. Berrett-Koehler Publishers, 1993.

CHAPTER 6
SUSTAINABLE HEALTHCARE

*"A ruined planet cannot sustain human lives in good health.
A healthy planet and healthy people are two sides of the
same coin."*

– Margaret Chan

6.1 INTRODUCTION

Climate change is one of the largest threats to human health and
well-being globally. Due to the impacts of climate change, our health
and our very existence are under threat. The healthcare industry is a
major consumer of natural resources, thereby contributing to the threat
to planetary health. Air pollution is associated with 31 adverse health
outcomes, including cancer and stroke. The healthcare industry itself
is a major contributor to pollution as well as the greenhouse gas (GHG)
emissions responsible for global warming and to the impoverishment
of the environment. The industry possesses a substantial and growing
environmental footprint due to a number of factors, including global
population growth, aging populations, and the rise of increasingly
energy and resource-intensive medical technologies. Each year 39
million people are pushed into poverty because of indebtedness to
cover healthcare costs. Healthcare has been estimated to account for
4.4% of global GHG emissions, with large variability between nations.
Figure 6.1 shows the impacts of climate change on human health [1].
The healthcare industry's contribution to global warming is counter to
the mission of improving health [2].

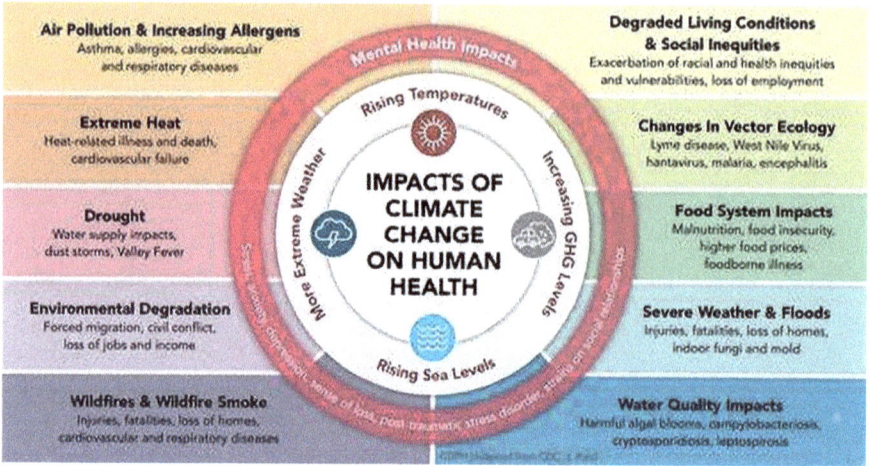

Figure 6.1 Impacts of climate change on human health [1].

Healthcare systems can be regarded as all the activities whose primary purpose is to promote, restore, and maintain health. They are supposed to protect and improve public health, but they are also socially and environmentally impactful structures which can cause negative side effects on the people's health. As healthcare systems face enormous challenges; sustainability is seen as a crucial requirement for making them fit for the future. Although healthcare accounts for approximately 10% of global economic output, healthcare systems have a considerable environmental impact. As our climate changes, healthcare systems and healthcare facilities come under mounting pressure. The health outcomes for patients and populations from healthcare systems are weighed against its environmental, social, and financial impacts to determine its overall sustainable value. Sustainability has become an important issue in a rapidly changing healthcare sector. The environment contributes to people's wellbeing, contributing to chronic diseases, such as asthma and cancer, or to acute illnesses like heat exhaustion. As the climate continues to change, risks to health systems and facilities (such hospitals, clinics and community care centers) are increasing, reducing the ability of health professionals to protect people from a range of climate hazards [3].

This chapter summarizes the healthcare sector's environmental footprint and the potential for reducing that footprint by applying the principles and tools of sustainability science. It begins with explaining healthcare systems. It presents the concepts of sustainability and sustainable healthcare. It covers sustainable healthcare principles. It provides some applications of sustainable healthcare. It highlights the benefits and challenges of sustainable healthcare. The last section concludes with comments.

6.2 HEALTHCARE SYSTEMS

Healthcare systems serve to protect and improve public health. Figure 6.2 shows the pyramid of healthcare needs, similar to Maslow's hierarchy of needs [4].

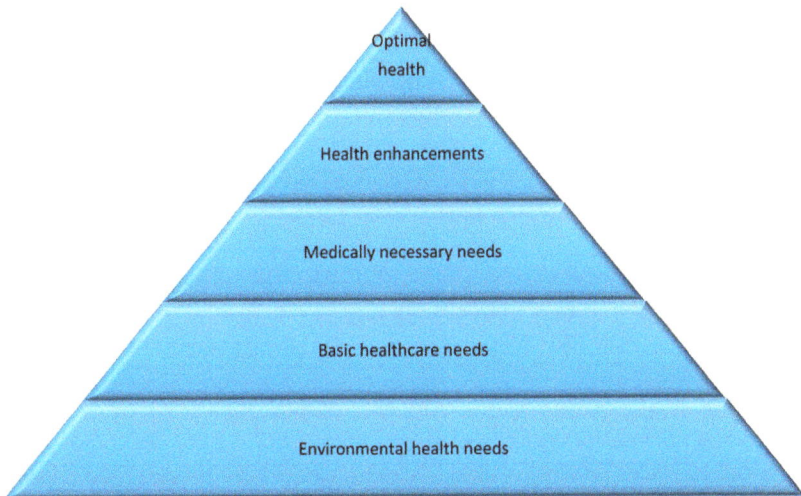

Figure 6.2 The pyramid of healthcare needs [4].

This pyramid, where lower needs take priority over higher ones, can be applied to both individuals and societies at different points in their development. The western world is approaching a pandemic in obesity and stress related illnesses, such as high blood pressure, heart disease, cancer and diabetes, good health is something we take for granted. Healthcare services enrich and prolong people's lives through health promotion and disease prevention and treatment. A successful health system has three attributes: healthy people, superior care, and fairness. It is a system that is fair to the health professionals, institutions, and businesses supporting and delivering care. A sustainable health system also has three key attributes: affordability, acceptability to key constituents, and adaptability. America's health system is neither as uccessful as it should be nor as sustainable as it must be. Figure 6.3 illustrates the various stakeholders and their functions in the healthcare system [5].

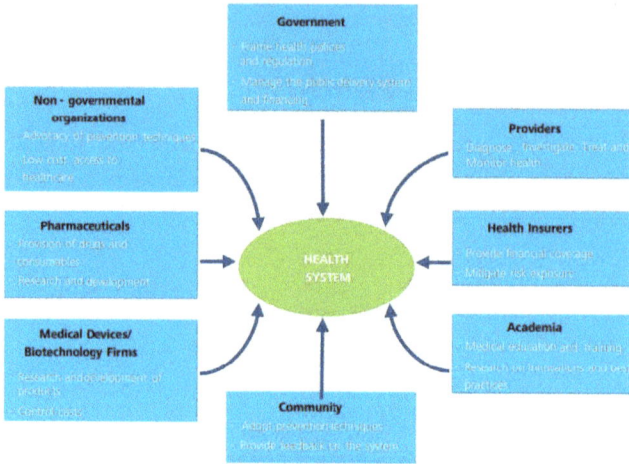

Figure 6.3 The various stakeholders and their functions in the healthcare system [5].

Some of the sources of inefficiency in US healthcare include the following [6]:

• Financial incentives that reward inefficiency (complications or readmissions)

• Dysfunctional competition rather than performance-based competition

• Insufficient involvement of patients in decision making (as in end-of-life care)

• Insufficient attention to prevention, disparities, primary care, health literacy, population health, and long-term results

• Administrative complexity of coping with multiple forms, regimens, and requirements of different insurers

• Regulatory regime that can only retard and not accelerate

innovation

• Distortions resulting from fraud, conflict of interest, and a dysfunctional malpractice system

The Commonwealth Fund periodically conducts a systematic comparison of health system performance in Australia, Canada, Germany, the Netherlands, New Zealand, Britain, and the United States. When assessed on the basis of various aspects of performance, including quality, access, efficiency, and equity, the United States came in last overall in 2010. The combination of high cost and relatively poor performance reflects inefficiency in the health system. To achieve a successful and sustainable health system, we must be able and willing to try many different things. We must be willing to adopt many strategies and use them to reach one big goal [6]. Everyone, including hospitals, needs to be a part of the solution and make changes that will help improve the environment.

Healthcare facilities are the frontline in protecting lives – but too often they are vulnerable to extreme weather events and long-term climate change. Health systems include an ensemble of all public and private organizations, institutions and resources mandated to improve, maintain or restore health as well as incorporate disease prevention. Sustainability has become an important issue for the public at large, for governments, and for the healthcare systems. It is related to the well-being of patients, healthcare employees, and the community. Environmentally sustainable health care facilities are those that improve, maintain or restore health, while minimizing negative impacts on the environment and leveraging opportunities to restore and improve. Facilities need to also optimize their use of natural resources, principally that of water and energy, ensuring a balance that is not too low to maintain good functioning, nor too high to waste and deplete resources.

6.3 CONCEPT OF SUSTAINABILITY

Sustainability, in one form or another, has been a concern for economists for well over 200 years. The concept of sustainability was originally coined in forestry, where it means never harvesting more than what the forest yields in new growth. The term "sustainability" has become popular in policy-oriented research as an expression of what public policies ought to achieve. The principal inspiration came from the Brundtland Report of 1987. Since then the concept has shifted in meaning [7]. The meaning of sustainability is constantly evolving in this rapidly changing world.

The "Three Pillars of Sustainability" describes what sustainable development is all about. This tool conveys that sustainability consists of environmental, social, and economic factors that are vital when discussing the topic. The pillars (or dimensions) are explained as follows [8,9]:

• *Environmental Sustainability* symbolizes the importance of things like natural resources and biodiversity to support life on Earth. This seems to be the most obvious pillar. Environmental sustainability is about the natural environment and how it remains productive and resilient to support human life. It occurs when humanity's rate of consumption does not exceed nature's rate of replenishment and when humanity's rate of generating pollution and emitting greenhouse gases does not exceed nature's rate of restoration.

• *Social Sustainability* places importance on social structures, well-being, and harmony; all factors that poverty, wars, and injustices can affect. It encompasses notions of equity, empowerment, accessibility, participation, cultural identity, and institutional stability. This is the ability of a society to uphold universal human rights and meet people's basic needs, such as healthcare, education, and transportation. Social sustainability is not about ensuring that everyone's needs are met. Rather, it aims at providing enabling conditions for everyone to have the capacity to realize their needs.

• *Economic Sustainability* implies a system of production that satisfies present consumption levels without compromising future needs. Economics is the study of the allocation of limited resources across unlimited wants. Economies consist of markets where transactions occur. We cannot have it all because there is not enough land, labor or capital (economic resources) to do so. Thus, we must decide what resources are best used to produce what goods [10]. Economic sustainability is the ability of human communities around the world to maintain their independence and have access to the resources required to meet their needs.

Sustainability creates and maintains the conditions under which humans and nature can exist in productive harmony, that permit fulfilling the social, economic, and other requirements of present and future generations. There is no hard and fast rule towards sustainability; it is a long-term process. Numerous practices are cited as threats to sustainability, such as political corruption, social inequality, the arms race, and profligate government expenditures. Health is central to the 2030 Agenda for Sustainable Development as it relates to many of the Sustainable Development Goals (SDGs) and is the specific focus of Goal 3. The health-related SDGs redefine the three functions of primary health care as: service provision, multisectoral actions, and the empowerment of citizens. Governments have recently reaffirmed their commitment to the SDGs.

6.4 WHAT IS SUSTAINABLE HEALTHCARE?

Healthcare professionals and administrators are responsible not only to follow best practices but also to manage environmental and economic impact for the benefit of the larger community. Hospitals, health practitioners, and laboratory community should lead the shift to carbon neutrality and to safer, more creative, and more viable goods and services. They can achieve this by decreasing their environmental footprint and implementing efficient approaches to address the effects of climate change and pollution without compromising the quality of healthcare.

Sustainability and healthcare are intricately related since the quality of our environment affects public health. From a clinical perspective, considering sustainability means allocating resources appropriately (both human and material) and considering the health and wellbeing of staff. In addition to the traditional pillars of sustainability (social, environmental and economic), we have systems sustainability in the context of healthcare as the fourth pillar, as shown in Figure 6.4 [9].

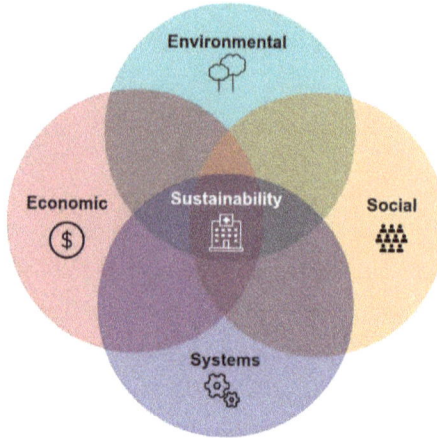

Figure 6.4 Four pillars of sustainability [11].

The healthcare system is regarded as a four-level framework: the patient, the care providers and staff, the organization, and the operations. Healthcare systems can be described as all the activities whose primary purpose is to promote, restore and maintain health. Figure 6.5 shows the sustainable healthcare system [4]. Healthcare systems need to address some key factors in order to develop towards sustainability. They can only be considered sustainable where all three elements (also termed "People, Planet and Profits") intersect and are upheld. In a sustainable healthcare system, the ecological environment must be recognized and addressed as a crucial factor.

Figure 6.5 Sustainable healthcare system [4].

Healthcare is a significant contributor to climate change and environmental degradation. The World Health Organization (WHO) has described climate change as the biggest health threat facing humanity, highlighting that those in low-income and disadvantaged communities are being affected first and hit the hardest. WHO defines an environmentally sustainable health care system "as a health system that improves, maintains or restores health, while minimizing negative impacts on the environment and leveraging opportunities to restore and improve it, to the benefit of the health and well-being of current and future generations" [12]. Sustainable healthcare is about understanding that our health and that of our environment around us are intrinsically linked. It refers to a system that meets the health needs of the present, without compromising the health of future generations. An environmentally sustainable health system is one that improves, maintains or restores health, while minimizing negative impacts on the environment.

6.5 SUSTAINABLE HEALTHCARE PRINCIPLES

In practice, sustainable healthcare is underpinned by three core principles [13]:

1.   *Sustainable Prevention:* Keeping people as healthy as possible

for as long as possible – and empowering them to take an active role in their health and wellbeing – reduces the risk of them becoming unwell

2.   *Sustainable Pathways:* When access to healthcare services is required, getting people to the right service at the right time and making healthcare pathways more efficient and joined-up can reduce healthcare's environmental footprint through reductions in patient travel.

3.   *Sustainable Practice:* When care or treatment is being delivered to patients, it is vital that the carbon footprint and wider environmental impacts of are kept to a minimum. Minimizing the environmental impact of care must not compromise the health outcomes or quality of care.

Sustainable health is a personal commitment to maintaining and taking responsibility for your own health, through preventative means. This implies having regular exercise, taking care of what we eat, and maintaining a healthy and balanced state of mind. Sustainable health is leading and maintaining a balanced life, by taking a "middle road" approach. Not too little, not too much is the key. The 10 principles of sustainable health [14]:

1. Maintain a balanced life, (middle road approach)

2. Have a healthy diet

3. Exercise regularly

4. Sleep well

5. Maintain a regular rhythm in life

6. Take preventative natural medicines to maintain health

7. Engage in spiritual practices manifested through meditation, mind training, and raising personal consciousness

8. Learn to live and laugh more

9. Build discipline in our selves through mind training and raising awareness

10. Take a simpler approach to life

The avenues for action for fostering environmental sustainability in health systems are the following [14]:

•   adopting a national environmental sustainability policy for health systems

•   minimizing and adequately managing waste and hazardous chemicals

•   promoting an efficient management of resources

•   promoting sustainable procurement

•   reducing health systems' emissions of greenhouse gases and air pollution

•   prioritizing disease prevention, health promotion and public health services

•   engaging the health workforce as an agent of sustainability

•   increasing community resilience and promoting local assets

•   creating incentives for change

•   promoting innovative models of care

Sustainable principles can be used to improve the quality of healthcare systems around the world.

6.6 APPLICATIONS OF SUSTAINABLE HEALTHCARE

Healthcare systems around the world are undergoing major changes in public policies to offer a better health service to their population. In healthcare, sustainability refers to the integration of environmental stewardship, social equity, and fiduciary responsibility to support healthy, equitable, and resilient environments. The following are some of the applications of sustainable healthcare [16]:

•   *Sustainable Hospitals:* Within the healthcare sector, hospitals account for the majority of CO2e emissions and there has been considerable research on improving sustainability outcomes for them. There is momentum for hospitals to reduce their ecological footprint and to decarbonize. Corporate sustainability is an important way to make hospitals more sustainable and competitive. The main objective for building sustainable healthcare facilities is [17]: (a) to enhance their capacity to protect and improve the health of their target communities in an unstable and changing climate; and (b) to empower them to optimize the use of resources and minimize the release of pollutants and waste into the environment. America's hospitals are working together to become more sustainable by adopting environmental, social, and economic practices. The sustainability of hospitals is crucial to promoting human well-being and health. Hospital buildings and laboratories can use renewable energy sources, including wind, solar photovoltaics, and solar thermal energy. Operating rooms are 3–6 times more energy intensive than the rest of the hospital. Renewable power sources should become the main sources of energy. An operating room can save thousands annually through sustainable procurement. Figure 6.6 shows the potential cost savings from sustainable procurement in hospitals (practice green health) [18].

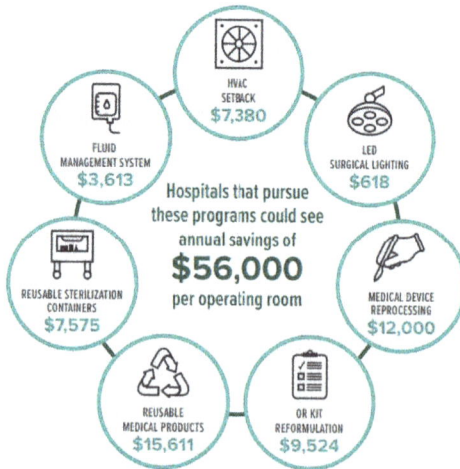

Figure 6.6 Potential cost savings from sustainable procurement in hospitals [18].

The medical facility shown in Figure 6.7 is located in Saint Vincent in the Caribbean, installed a renewable energy system to improve its access to reliable energy [19].

Figure 6.7 A medical facility uses a renewable energy [19].

• *Sustainable Laboratories:* There is a relationship between laboratory strategies and sustainability. Sustainable thinking has already been introduced in the medical laboratory community. Sustainability could be applied to reduce the environmental impact of clinical laboratories by ensuring that resources are used efficiently and responsibly. Laboratory medicine can contribute to a sustainable healthcare system through integration of innovation and emerging technologies while providing high-quality services to patients and caregivers. Clinical laboratories can establish sustainable development goals and reduce their environmental impact. They use far more energy and water than a typical office building. Thus, there is a need to adopt good environmental practices in clinical laboratories. Emerging technologies in clinical laboratories (such as telemedicine, e-health, and mobile health) can play a role in disease prevention and thus healthcare sustainability.

• *Sustainable Waste Management:* An important issue to be tackled regarding sustainability in the healthcare sector is the management of waste disposal and air pollution. Medical waste can be classified as hazardous or non-hazardous (general) waste. Hazardous medical waste is 15% of all medical waste generated and can cause diseases and environmental hazards. Medical waste problems are due to lack of awareness and willingness on the part of healthcare employees and ambiguous policies and laws about proper management of medical waste. With the increasing concerns regarding contagious and infectious diseases, due to climate change as well as resistance to medications and treatments, the effective management of medical waste has become a strategic priority for healthcare providers [20]. Improper healthcare waste management can occur for several reasons, such as lack of awareness about the health hazards related to health care waste, inadequate training in proper waste management, lack of infrastructure or energy, and lack of appropriate regulations or enforcement of existing regulations. Medical waste has become one of the top pollutant sources worldwide and is a major factor affecting disease spread and air, water, and soil quality in and around healthcare structures. Sustainable practices in healthcare waste disposal should be implemented. Holding of meetings, seminars, conferences, and other events virtually can also help reduce carbon emissions and footprints to a great extent. Healthcare institutions generally use disposable products to minimize infection while treating patients. Figure 6.8 shows medical waste disposal [21].

Figure 6.8 Medical waste [21]

•   *Green Surgery:* Operating theatres contribute towards carbon emissions as significant users of medical equipment and supplies. The surgical community recognized the value of sustainable healthcare for surgical conditions: to share and promote ways of practicing that are less harmful to the environment and to continue to transform surgery for the future. Within surgical services there are opportunities for ensuring lean surgical pathways, including identifying and avoiding unnecessary procedures or unused single-use items in surgery. The green or sustainable surgery challenge in UK is illustrated in Figure 6.9 [22].

Figure 6.9 The Green surgery challenge in UK [23].

Other areas of application of sustainable healthcare include sustainable dentistry, sustainable anesthetic, medical transportation, sustainable workplace, pharmacology, psychology, ambulances, and burials

6.7 BENEFITS

Great strides have been made in improving people's health in recent years. Climate change is the biggest global health threat of the 21st century. Sustainability in healthcare is based on a simple principle: Everything that humans need for their survival and well-being depends on the natural environment. Digital technology routinely may bring broader societal and environmental benefits, but may lead to unnecessary risk to all if not embedded. The Race to Zero initiative has also seen health-care systems across 18 countries, including state-level systems within the US, commit to reducing emissions. The UK's National Health Service (NHS) was the first healthcare system to commit to reaching net zero carbon emissions. The NHS and Public Health England lead the world in sustainable health care. Other benefits of sustainable healthcare include the following [23].

1.   *Caring for the Patients:* One way in which hospitals are looking to implement sustainable practices is through their patient care. Caring for people and caring for the planet are two sides of the same coin. Sustainability needs to become an integral part of how care providers operate.

2.   *Investing in Technology:* Sustainability initiatives often go hand-in-hand with technology advancements, where switching to reusable items instead of single use offers environmental benefits and cost savings. For example, telehealth capabilities help to improve the green credentials of hospitals by reducing patient travel at the same time as extending the reach of care for those who struggle to access it. Investing in technology is investing in sustainability.

3.   *Better Care Lowers Environmental Footprint:* Healthcare is one of the world's most polluting industries. There is growing motivation among the healthcare community to reduce the negative environmental impact of healthcare. Reducing the carbon footprint of healthcare requires direct action to reduce waste, increase energy efficiency, adopt circular practices, and extend access. But it also requires the radical reform of care pathways. Healthcare without Harm is a nongovernmental organization (NGO) that aims to reduce the environmental impact of healthcare around the world. It seeks to transform global healthcare so that the sector reduces its environmental footprint and becomes a leader in the global movement for environmental health and justice.

6.8 CHALLENGES

Good health for all in our time requires handling of a number of challenges: demographic changes, empowerment of citizens, changing illness patterns, traumatic events and organizational coordination. The societal challenges evolving from global health are complex and require commitment and engagement from multiple perspectives [24]. Sustainable healthcare continues to attract controversy around the world. Inequalities continue to be a fundamental challenge for universal health coverage, which aims to ensure that everyone can access quality health services without facing financial hardship. The management of test ordering to monitor chronic diseases in primary care can also improve overall healthcare quality and reduce cost. Other challenges include [1,18,25]:

•   *Awareness:* A lack of awareness about sustainability among clinical laboratory employees is currently one of the most commonly barriers for sustainability in healthcare. Being environmentally aware and accountable is something that is increasingly being demanded by our society. National and international scientific societies have a fundamental role to play in reducing this awareness gap by providing educational materials and conducting continuing education sessions. This should increase awareness about sustainability in healthcare from a holistic point of view.

•   *Unnecessary Tests:* A revision of the existing laboratory test ordering policy and avoidance of unnecessary laboratory tests would strongly contribute to healthcare sustainability. It is important to have optimization and standardization of blood test ordering for monitoring chronic conditions.

•   *Energy:* Energy use in clinics can be reduced through energy efficiency measures and behavior change. Examples of behavior changes include turning off computer monitors overnight, turning off lights and machines when not needed, using low-power lighting, and agreeing to run air-conditioning/heating as needed. For clinics that are not within a larger complex, installing solar on the roof will decrease electricity used.

•   *Water:* Much of the health care delivery in developing countries still takes place in settings with inadequate or non-existent municipal water supply or water and wastewater treatment facilities. In many nations, it is mandatory to reduce biological loading, and then treat the water in a municipal system. However, this is not always possible in rural areas where no service is available or in cities where the municipality requires on-site treatment.

•   *Healthcare Waste:* Over half of the world's population is estimated to be at risk from environmental, occupational or public health threats resulting from improperly treated health care waste.

Reducing waste from a healthcare setting has been shown to be one of the more effective measures a facility can take to help decarbonize. Reduction and efficient management of medical waste ensures healthcare hygiene and safety of employees and communities, and controls pollution through reduction or prevention of harmful emissions. As climate change, air pollution, plastic waste, and medical waste threaten human health and environmental sustainability.

•   *Chemicals:* An estimated 1.6 million lives were lost in 2016 due to exposure to selected chemicals. Chemicals are used for unique purposes, such as in chemotherapy to treat cancer, or as disinfectants for cleaning and sterilization. In addition, many medical devices such as thermometers, which contain mercury, are still in use.

•   *Radiation:* Direct patient exposure to ionizing radiation during medical procedures constitutes the largest anthropogenic source of population radiation exposure overall. The majority of healthcare emissions relate to the healthcare supply chain, including the production, transport, and disposal of goods.

•   *Air Quality:* Healthcare contributes to air pollution and greenhouse gases (GHGs) through energy consumption (transport, electricity, heating, and cooling) as well as product manufacture, use, and disposal. Ambient air pollution, which is principally driven by fossil fuel combustion, kills an estimated 4.2 million people annually. Its health impacts, which include damage to the heart, lungs, and every other vital organ, are exacerbated by climate change.

•   *Food:* Climate threats to health systems are particularly disruptive for individuals and communities when they affect health care facilities (HCFs). Iin many nations, HCFs are major consumers of food and can therefore model and promote health and sustainability through their food choices. An HCF can reduce its GHGs and become more resilient to electricity grid disruptions and unreliability.

•   *Leadership:* A health system that is socially, environmentally, and financially sustainable requires clinical leadership. Few healthcare workers possess the practical skills for creating new models of care. Practical skills for the transition to environmentally sustainable health care are not commonly known by or taught to healthcare professionals. Educating and training the healthcare workforce has been identified as a key priority for the transition to environmentally sustainable healthcare. There is a concern that medical educators may not be sufficiently informed to teach students well about sustainable healthcare.

• *Healthcare Facilities:* These provide an interesting challenge, as they often include specific design constraints that are highly regulated and materially intensive. Reduction of the embodied carbon of building materials is a major focus to decarbonize the built environment. In new clinical infrastructure, the baseline goal is net-zero energy or net negative emissions. Increasing the longevity and life span of the healthcare facilities would reduce the need for future construction. In the US, the Energy Star program provides accounting tools for estimating energy use of individual healthcare facilities.

• *Decarbonization Cost:* Another challenge to reducing carbon emissions in the healthcare sector is the lack of information on the cost of carbon emissions and the cost of decarbonization interventions. Such science-based knowledge is critical input in cost-benefit analyses in designing decarbonization strategies. The social cost of carbon is largely uncertain. Tracking the cost of decarbonization techniques is a prerequisite for allocating limited healthcare resources.

6.9 CONCLUSION

As healthcare systems face enormous challenges, sustainability is regarded as a crucial requirement for making them fit for the future. The healthcare industry has begun to embrace a sustainability mindset as the linkage between greener operations, improved health care, and lower operating costs is becoming more apparent. Sustainable healthcare may be regarded as healthcare services of better quality, more affordable, with less impact on the planet, and that can be accessed by people equally and efficiently. It should be able to avoid unnecessary treatment and inadequate use of resources. To pursue sustainability is to create and maintain the conditions under which humans and nature can coexist in productive harmony. The most cost-effective way to achieve sustainable health care is to keep people healthy.

Sustainable healthcare in medical education remains a relatively novel concept. It is now a General Medical Council requirement to incorporate education for sustainable healthcare into medical curricula, emphasizing the need to close the gap between educational rhetoric and action [26]. Since quality improvement is an increasingly feature in health professions education, this presents a ripe opportunity for integrating sustainability into the curriculum in a meaningful and practical way.

Although there has been some progress on improving global health in recent years, there is a long way to go for environment-friendly hospitals, healthcare systems, and clinical laboratories to become the norm. Sustainability practices should be an essential element of healthcare's strategic business plans. For more information on sustainable healthcare, one should consult books in [27-42] and the following related journals:

- *Sustainability*
- *Sustainable Hospitals*
- *Sustainability Analytics and Modeling*
- *Future Healthcare Journal.*

REFERENCE

[1]   "Public health services climate change and health,"

https://www.sandiegocounty.gov/hhsa/programs/phs/climate-change-and-public-health.html

[2]   H. Hu et al., "Sustainability in health care," Annual Review of Environment and Resources, vol. 47, July 2022, pp. 173-196.

[3]   M. N. O. Sadiku, P. O. Adebo, and J. O. Sadiku, "Sustainable healthcare," submitted to a journal.

[4]   M. Fischer, "Fit for the future? A new approach in the debate about what makes healthcare systems really sustainable," Sustainability, vol. 7, no. 1, 2015, pp. 294-312.

[5]   "Innovative and sustainable healthcare management: Strategies for growth,"

https://www2.deloitte.com/content/dam/Deloitte/in/Documents/life-sciences-health-care/in-lshc-innovative-healthcare-noexp.pdf

[6]   H. V. Fineberg, "A successful and sustainable health system — How to get there from here," The New England Journal of Medicine, vol. 366, March 2012.

https://www.nejm.org/doi/full/10.1056/NEJMsa1114777

[7]   T. Kuhlman and J. Farrington, "What is sustainability?" Sustainability, vol. 2, 2010, pp. 3436-3448.

[8]   A. Browne, "Explainer: What is sustainability and why is it important?" October 2022,

https://earth.org/what-is-sustainability/

[9]   "What is sustainability?"

https://www.mcgill.ca/sustainability/files/sustainability/what-is-sustainability.pdf

[10]   S. R. Elliot, "Sustainability: An economic perspective," Resources, Conservation and Recycling, vol. 44, no. 3, June 2005, pp.

263-277.

[11]   S. Blanch and D. Anderson, "Healthcare sustainability,"

https://www.ache.org/blog/2021/designing-for-healthcare-sustainability-a-framework

[12]   "Sustainable healthcare," Wikipedia, the free encyclopedia, https://en.wikipedia.org/wiki/Sustainable_Healthcare

[13]   "What is sustainable healthcare?" December 2022,

https://www.bupa.com/news/stories-and-insights/2022/what-is-sustainable-healthcare#:~:text=It%20describes%20a%20system%20that%20meets%20the%20health,way%20that%20supports%20both%20people%20and%20planet%20health.

[14]   "Sustainable health,"

https://www.sustainable-development.net/information/PDF/050428HE-Sustainable_Health.pdf

[15]   "Environmentally sustainable health systems: A strategic document," February 2017,

https://www.who.int/publications/i/item/WHO-EURO-2017-2241-41996-57723

[16]   A. Molero et al., "Sustainability in healthcare: Perspectives and reflections regarding laboratory medicine," Annals of Laboratory Medicine, vol. 41, no. 2, March 2021, pp. 139–144.

[17]   C. Corvalan et al., Towards Climate Resilient and Environmentally Sustainable Health Care Facilities," International Journal of Environmental Research and Public Health, vol. 17, no. 23, November 2020.

[18]   "Sustainable procurement in health care guide,"

https://practicegreenhealth.org/sites/default/files/202007/Sustainable%20procurement%20guide%20%28U.S.%20version%29.pdf

[19] "WHO publishes guidance on climate resilient and environmentally sustainable health care facilities," October 2020,

https://www.who.int/news/item/12-10-2020-who-publishes-guidance-on-climate-resilient-and-environmentally-sustainable-health-care-facilities

[20]   S. M. Lee and D. Lee, "Effective medical waste management for sustainable green healthcare," International Journal of Environmental Research and Public Health, vol. 19, no. 22, November 2022.

[21]   "10 Best sustainable healthcare innovations,"

https://thelifesciencesmagazine.com/sustainable-healthcare-innovations/

[22]   "Green surgery challenge"

https://sustainablehealthcare.org.uk/what-we-do/green-surgery-challenge

[23]   "Three reasons why sustainable hospitals deliver better care," June 2021,

https://www.philips.com/a-w/about/news/archive/blogs/innovation-matters/2021/20210610-three-reasons-why-sustainable-hospitals-deliver-better-care.html

[24]   "Linnaeus knowledge environment: Sustainable health,"

https://lnu.se/en/meet-linnaeus-university/knowledge-environments/sustainable-health/

[25]   D. Duindam, "Transitioning to sustainable healthcare: Decarbonising healthcare clinics, a literature review," Challenges, vol. 13, no. 2, 2022.

[26]   D. Gupta, L. Shantharam, and B. K. MacDonald, "Sustainable healthcare in medical education: Survey of the student perspectives at a UK medical school," BMC Medical Education, vol. 22, 2022.

[27]   K. Schroeder et al., Sustainable Healthcare. John Wiley & Sons, 2012.

[28]   R. Guenther and G. Vittori, Sustainable Healthcare Architecture. Wiley 2013.

[29]   C. R. Rich, J. K. Singleton, and S. S. Wadhwa, Sustainability

for Healthcare Management: A Leadership Imperative. Routledge/Earthscan, 2013

[30]   A. B. Shani, C. G. Worley, and S. A. Mohrman (eds.), Organizing for Sustainable Healthcare. Emerald Group Publishing Limited, 2012.

[31]   P. A, Morgon, Sustainable Development for the Healthcare Industry: Reprogramming the Healthcare Value Chain. Springer, 2014.

[32]   E. Lettieri et al. (eds.), Improving Sustainability During Hospital Design and Operation: A Multidisciplinary Evaluation Tool. Springer, 2015.

[33]   A. B. Shani and S. A. Mohrman, Reconfiguring the Eco-System for Sustainable Healthcare. Emerald Group Publishing Limited, 2014.

[34]   B. Y. F. Fong, Systems Thinking and Sustainable Healthcare Delivery. Taylor & Francis, 2022

[35]   Institute of Medicine, Green Healthcare Institutions: Health, Environment, and Economics: Workshop Summary. National Academies Press, 2007.

[36]   S. Trobiani, Sustainable Healthcare Reform. BookBaby, 2013.

[37]   S. Lennane, Creating Community Health: Interventions for Sustainable Healthcare. Taylor & Francis, 2023.

[38]   M. Abdel-Basset, R. K. Chakrabortty, and A. Gamal, Multi-Criteria Decision Making Theory and Applications in Sustainable Healthcare. Boca Raton, FL: CRC Press, 2023.

[39]   A. Ng, B. Fong, and P. Yuen (eds.), Sustainable Health and Long-Term Care Solutions for an Aging Population. IGI Global, 2107.

[40]   J. Broerse and J. Grin (eds.), Toward Sustainable Transitions in Healthcare Systems. Taylor & Francis, 2017.

[41]   W. A. Haseltine, Affordable Excellence: The Singapore Healthcare Story: How to Create and Manage Sustainable Healthcare Systems. Brookings Institution Press, 2013.

[42] K. Schroeder et al., Sustainable Healthcare. Wiley, 2012.

CHAPTER 7
SUSTAINABLE MANUFACTURING

"If it can't be reduced, reused, repaired, rebuilt, refurbished, refinished, resold, recycled, or composted, then it should be restricted, designed, or removed from production."

– Peter Seeger

7.1 INTRODUCTION

Manufacturing is the main pillar of the modern society. It is a well-acknowledged fact that traditional manufacturing processes are generally designed for high performance and low cost with little attention paid to environmental issues. Although manufacturing systems create material wealth, they consume a great amount of resources and generate a lot of waste, which is responsible for the degradation of the environment. Thus, such traditional manufacturing processes have retained the negative image of being inefficient, polluting, and harmful. Manufacturers are under pressure by regulations and consumers to reduce the environmental impact of their activities.

Today, humans are consuming natural resources through manufacturing activities at an alarming rate, which is not sustainable. For example, between 1950 and 2005, worldwide metals production grew six fold, oil consumption eight fold, and natural gas consumption 14-fold. The current assumption of unlimited resources and unlimited world's capacity for regeneration is no longer acceptable. Thus, minimizing the resource consumption and reducing the environmental impact of manufacturing systems has become very important [1].

Sustainable manufacturing (SM) is manufacturing products through economically-sound processes that minimize negative environmental impacts while conserving energy and natural resources. The goal of sustainable manufacturing is to minimize waste, maximize resource efficiency, and reduce the environmental impact of manufacturing. It is imperative that manufacturing processes should consider sustainability at every level, so that there will be comprehensive adherence to sustainability principles. Properly implemented, sustainable manufacturing can lead to several advantages [2].

This chapter describes sustainable manufacturing and how environmental sustainability helps in achieving it. It begins by explaining the concept of sustainability. It discusses what sustainable manufacturing is all about. It covers some sustainable approaches. It provides some examples of sustainable manufacturing. It highlights the benefits and challenges of SM. It covers the global adoption of SM. The last section concludes with comments.

7.2 THE CONCEPT OF SUSTAINABILITY

Sustainability is the future of manufacturing. It has been a keyword in the 21st century because it is one of the global grand challenges. For example, we hear about sustainable engineering, sustainable development, sustainable energy, sustainable software, sustainable design, sustainable living, economic sustainability, social sustainability, ecological sustainability, etc. In this same way, there has been considerable discussion about green chemistry, green engineering, green business, green manufacturing, green food, green economy, green energy, etc. The two terms (sustainability and green) are often used interchangeably. Sustainable development has been a major driving initiative in engineering businesses throughout the world. Green engineering involves creating healthy living environments that use natural resources wisely and conservatively [3].

Sustainability requires monitoring your operation and continually looking for ways to improve. It has been applied to many areas including manufacturing, engineering, design, and business. It will be a crucial issue for the present and future generation of manufacturing solutions. When we talk about sustainability, we often mention the three Ps: people, planet, profit, as shown in Figure 7.1 [4].

Figure 7.1 The three Ps of sustainability: people, planet, profit [4].

The pillars of sustainability are a powerful tool for defining the sustainability problem. These consist of at least the economic, social, and environmental pillars, shown in Figure 7.2 [5].

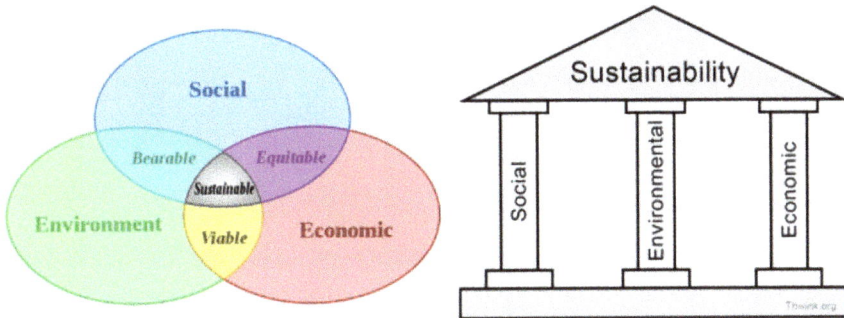

Figure 7.2 The three pillars of sustainability [5]

The four pillars of sustainability analysis are energy, efficiency, environment, and society. Sustainability analysis is multi-disciplinary in nature. It requires approaches from different disciplines such as manufacturing engineering, environmental engineering, optimization, social science, and finance. Sustainability starts with green manufacturing and extends to industrial networks and then to the ecosystem. Sustainability of a system is its ability to survive and retain its functionality over time. A distinctly sustainable society is capable of surviving and prospering indefinitely [6].

Today, sustainability is seen in three-dimensions: environmental, economic, and socio-cultural, which are illustrated in Figure 7.3 and explained as follows [7].

Figure 7.3 Sustainability in the interaction of environment, social actions, and economics [7].

• *Environmental Sustainability:* The earth's resources and processes are connected with human societies. Environmental sustainability describes a possible way that human societies can sustainably develop by living within the system earth and using the resources of planet earth. It is focused on three protection goals: protection of human health, resources, and the ecosystem.

• *Economic Sustainability:* This addresses effective investments, finance, job creation, and competitiveness.

• *Social Sustainability:* This addresses equity, justice, security, employment, and participation.

7.3 WHAT IS SUSTAINABLE MANUFACTURING?

Sustainable manufacturing (SM) (or green manufacturing) can be defined as a method for manufacturing that minimizes waste and reduces the environmental impact. These goals will be obtained mainly by adopting practices that will influence the product design, process design, and operational principles. Therefore, sustainable manufacturing may be regarded as an approach that integrates product and process that will consider sustainability at all levels of the life cycle of manufacturing: product, process, and system. It promotes eliminating production and processing wastes through eco-efficient practices and encourages adopting new environmental technologies. The six major elements significantly affecting the sustainability of manufacturing processes are shown in Figure 7.4 [8].

Figure 7.4 Six major elements affecting the sustainability of manufacturing processes [8].

Sustainable manufacturing involves developing sustainable products with total life-cycle considerations. It is the creation of manufactured products using non-polluting, natural resources conservation practices, supported by economically sound and safe manufacturing processes, practices and systems. Such manufacturing practices are safe and are economically sound while simultaneously being societally beneficial.

Sustainable manufacturing requires that all manufacturers should aim for the following four activities that would help the environment across its entire supply chain [1]: (1) Energy use reduction, (2) Water use reduction, (3) Emissions reduction, (4) Waste generation reduction. Sustainable manufacturing should integrate the sustainable activities at all levels of manufacturing – product, process, and system. This may involve the following 9R: reduce, reuse, recycle, recover, redesign, remanufacturing, repurpose, refurbish, and refuse. Industry 4.0 provides opportunities for the realization of sustainable manufacturing. Figure 7.5 shows the key contributors to sustainable manufacturing [9].

Figure 7.5 Key contributors to sustainable manufacturing [9].

Sustainable manufacturing is causing companies to implement new design and analysis procedures, energy reduction methods, material reduction efforts, and improved materials handling practices. Reducing consumption of energy, raw materials, water, and other resources in a factory to leverage greater efficiency and productivity is challenging and often starts with the basics of switching off lights and replacing the luminaires with LEDs. Fabric waste is turned into tiles and furniture.

Sustainable manufacturing has become the most important aspect to be considered by all manufacturing engineers otherwise known as production engineers, because it is an obligation to the world we live in. The three major principles sustainabilty leaders, actors and implementers should keep in mind are reducing the resource utilization, using environment-friendly materials, and reducing all forms of waste, while advocating for the reuse and recycling of materials.

The manufacturing industry seeks indicators to measure sustainability of manufactured products and manufacturing processes. The main tool commonly used to implement SM is the Life Cycle Assessment (LCA). It is a method used in assessing environmental impacts associated with all the stages of a product's life, from cradle to grave. It is an approach to examine fully the environmental impact of different activities performed by humans including the production of goods and services by corporations. LCA is mainly concerned with identifying the environmental impact of a given product or process at each stage of their life.

7.4 SUSTAINABLE APPROACHES

The issue of sustainability is becoming more and more central to the industry. Manufacturers engaged in sustainability activities include those of all sizes, ages and sectors. The reasons companies are pursuing sustainability goals and initiatives include [10]:

- Increase operational efficiency by reducing costs and waste

- Respond to or reach new customers and increase competitive advantage

- Protect and strengthen brand and reputation and build public trust

- Build long-term business viability and success

- Respond to regulatory constraints and opportunities

Ways that companies progress further on the path to sustainability include [10]:

Address sustainability in a coordinated, integrated and formal manner, rather than in an ad hoc, unconnected, and informal manner

Focus on increased competitiveness and revenues rather than primarily focusing on cost-cutting, risk reduction, and improved efficiency

- Use innovation, scenario planning, and strategic analysis to go beyond compliance

- Integrate sustainability across business functions

- Focus more on the long term

- Work collaboratively with external stakeholders

Companies can build sustainable manufacturing for the new normal. To practice sustainable manufacturing in your company requires the following steps [11]:

1. Start practicing sustainable manufacturing with a plan.

2. Keep the benefits at the forefront of your focus.

3. Get certified in ISO standards that encourage environmental sustainability.

4. Analyze your production process and see what can be eliminated.

5. Encourage your entire company to be involved.

7.5 SUSTAINABLE MANUFACTURING EXAMPLES

Sustainable manufacturing is the creation of manufactured products using economically-sound, non-polluting processes which minimize negative environmental impacts while conserving energy and natural resources as well as increasing productivity and efficiency. It is relevant in different sectors like business, economics, environment, and society. Some examples of sustainable manufacturing include [12-14]:

- *Automotive Industry:* The automotive industry is regarded as a major economic force worldwide. It has undergone substantial transformations, which have reduced fuel consumption, minimized environmental impact, and improved safety. Sustainable manufacturing in the automotive industry is becoming an imperative strategy to drive profitable growth and provide value to customers. As the automotive industry continues to embrace and make Sustainability its strategic imperative, it is important that automotive organizations reflect the newer 3P definition of sustainability: Pollution Prevention Pays [15].

In 2008 GM, a multinational corporation, approved three sustainability metrics: an energy use index, a water index, and a carbon emission index to calculate the company's performance and targets. Ford strove to eliminate waste from production. BMW was rated the world's most sustainable company in 2016.

•   *Construction Industry:* The construction industry has its footprints on all human efforts to control, modify, and dominate nature and natural systems. There is a growing consensus that delivering a sustainability culture and environment starts with incorporating sustainability thoughts at the planning and design stages of an infrastructure construction project. Geotechnical engineering can significantly influence the sustainability of infrastructure development because of its early position in the construction process [16].

•   *Furniture Manufacturing:* A furniture production company can integrate sustainability concepts in order to make a positive impact on the environment, society and its own financial success. The principles of lean and green manufacturing can deliver a significant, positive impact on multiple measures of operational performance of furniture production [17].

•   *Pharmaceutical Manufacturing:* This relies on resources such as energy and water that can be expensive and generate large amounts of waste both toxic and benign. A robust focus on corporate sustainability can benefit pharmaceutical manufacturers. A sustainability strategy that focuses on managing risks associated with water use, energy consumption, and waste can prevent FDA warning letters [18].

•   *Chemical Manufacturing:* Chemical manufacturing produces a large amount of wastes and also carbon emissions that harm the environment. Any process that reduces carbon emissions improves the sustainability of operations. Fossil fuels can be replaced with renewable energy sources in chemical manufacturing to facilitate sustainable production of high quality chemicals [19].

•   *Customized Manufacturing:* The production of personalized products using sustainable manufacturing systems and supply chains allows localized manufacturing and therefore a shortening of supply chains becoming more energy and resource efficient. Reshoring the apparel manufacturing to allow for faster, more customizable fashion would redefine the interaction between the manufacturer and the consumer. It is expected that this shift to more localized manufacturing will primarily affect goods manufacturers [20].

•   *Remanufacturing:* This involves the processing of used products for restoration to their original condition. Remanufacturing and product recovery attracts significant attention due to environmental concerns, legislative requirements, consumer interests in green products and market image of manufacturers.

•   *Resource Conservation:* The pressing needs of energy, water, and other resource conservation worldwide is a major engineering challenge. The most recent data on water use in the US reported manufacturers consumed approximately 21 billion gallons per day from both municipal and self-supplied sources. As drivers such as population growth and climate change increase pressure on freshwater resources, both at the local and global level, manufacturers are seeking ways to incorporate more efficient and sustainable water use practices into their operations. This sustainable water use is driven from both an environmental perspective and a business perspective.

•   *Sustainable Logistics:* Transportation is an important part of the manufacturing supply chains. There is a need for a sustainable means for shipping goods from origin A to destination B. Sustainable shipping works towards reducing transportation emissions footprint that can be harmful to the environment [21].

•   *Regulatory Compliance:* A sustainability strategy that focuses on managing risks associated with water use, energy consumption, and waste can prevent FDA warning letters.

7.6 BENEFITS

Environmental responsibility has become an integral part of the way products are manufactured, marketed, and purchased. The benefits of sustainable manufacturing are almost infinite. An increasing number of manufacturers are realizing substantial benefits from sustainable business practices. Some forward-thinking organizations have added vice presidents of sustainability to their leadership teams. Designing products to be environmentally benign can contribute to their successful introduction and maintenance. Other benefits of sustainable manufacturing include the following [22,23].

•   *Increase Sales:* Sustainable manufacturing will make your business more attractive and marketable. Sustainability should be particularly profitable for manufacturers.

•   *Energy Efficiency:* Companies of all sizes are pursuing sustainability by improving efficiency and reducing their energy consumption. When manufacturing focuses on efficiency, energy use invariably decreases.

•   *Save Energy Costs:* Replacing incandescent bulbs and fluorescent tubes with LED lighting can reduce electricity usage because LED lighting consumes a smaller amount of electricity. Converting to a renewable energy source, such as wind, geothermal or solar, can stabilize energy cost with a much longer payback period.

•   *Incentives:* There are government incentives, tax credits, grants and utility company rebates for businesses that support sustainable practices.

•   *Workplace Morale:* Implement green practices typically spurs collaboration and teamwork.

•   *Recycling of Waste:* Implementing sustainable practices in manufacturing reduces water and energy usage, minimizes waste and decreases hazardous emissions. Production waste is collected by the manufacturing company or by a specialized recycling company and returned for recycling.

•   *Environmental Health and Safety:* Sustainable manufacturing enhances the safety of the products, employees, and community. Safety practices include developing and enforcing employee safety procedures. Such practices can return your investment by providing an accident-free workplace and demonstrating to your employees that their health and safety are important.

•   *Quality Improvement:* Quality improvement programs offer your best employee-driven opportunities for enhanced teamwork while registering satisfied customers, sales growth, and efficient operation.

•   Reduce costs, reduce waste, increase operational efficiency

- Increase competitive advantage

- Enhance brand name recognition and reputation while simultaneously cultivating public trust and loyalty

- Contribute to long-term business visibility, viability and success

- Comply with regulatory constraints

Some of these benefits are illustrated in Figure 7.6.

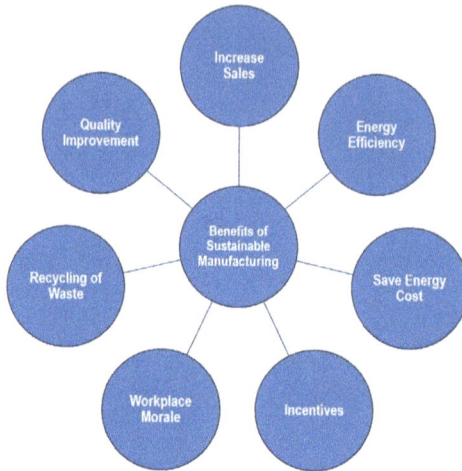

Figure 7.6 Some benefits of sustainable manufacturing.

Other benefits of sustainable manufacturing include improved morale, improved brand value, lowered regulatory concerns, increased market opportunities, improved product performance, and decreased liabilities. SM considers the cost of compliance to the environmental guidance prescribed in relation to the value to society and the adverse impact imposed on society and the manufacturing industry, such as job flight to foreign low wage jurisdictions, caused by the prescribed sustainability regulation(s).

7.7 CHALLENGES

The major challenges faced by the manufacturing industry in its pursuit of sustainability goals are as follows [24].

1.   The manufacturing industry is facing the challenge of measuring sustainability performance in a product's life cycle. Developing metrics for sustainable manufacturing is critical to enable manufacturing companies to quantitatively measure the sustainability performance in specific manufacturing processes.

2.   Industry is unable to measure economic, social, and environmental impacts and costs of their products accurately during the entire life cycle and across their supply chain.

3.   Full life cycle analysis or assessment (LCA) of products requires new methods to analyze, integrate, and aggregate information across hierarchical levels, organizational entities, and supply chain participants. Existing methods of aggregation do not take into account sustainability issues.

4.   Cost is one of the main reasons manufacturers stay away from sustainable practices.

5.   Industry lacks neutral and trusted standards and programs to demonstrate, deploy, and accredit new sustainable manufacturing practices, guidelines and methods.

6.   Regulations need to be supported and informed by industry standards. These regulations/standards should be harmonized.

7.   Current manufacturing modeling and assessment criteria require intensive revisions and upgrades to keep up with these new challenges.

8.   The production and delivery of personalized goods and services using sustainable manufacturing systems and processes presents a major challenge.

9.   The word "sustainability" has been overused and abused.

10.   Consumer education is needed and in some cases critical, as some customers are not sure what packaging can and cannot be recycled.

11.   There are too many metrics; these can be condensed and grouped, predicated on consolidation and harmonization.

7.8 GLOBAL ADOPTION OF SUSTAINABLE MANUFACTURING

With Goal 12 of the UN Sustainable Development Goals encouraging responsible production, sustainable practices have been gaining traction worldwide. An increasing number of organizations are treating "sustainability" as an important part of their strategy to increase growth and global competitiveness. Manufacturers around the world are making the move toward adopting sustainability. We now consider how different nations are integrating sustainability into their manufacturing and design.

• *United States:* Figure 7.7 shows environmental impact of the US manufacturing industry [25]. The US Environmental Protection Agency (EPA) describes sustainable manufacturing as "the creation of manufactured products through economically-sound processes that minimize negative environmental impacts while conserving energy and natural resources. Sustainable manufacturing also enhances employee, community and product as well as process safety."

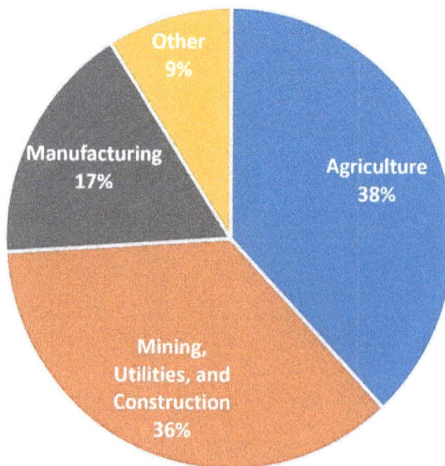

Figure 7.7 Environmental impact of the US manufacturing industry (modified) [25].

While the manufacturing industry is a driving force of the American economy, it also has a sizable carbon footprint. In recent times, there has been renewed interest in US manufacturing and endeavors launched for sustainable manufacturing initiatives. For example. the Kentucky Sustainable Manufacturing Initiative (KSMI) is designed to assist manufacturers with learning how to integrate sustainability into their daily manufacturing operations.

• *United Kingdom:* It has been recommended that food and drink manufacturers become key agents of change. In response to this, Coca-Cola Enterprises (CCE) has released the final findings, entitled Sustainable Manufacturing for the Future. It has launched a £56m operational investment plan, accelerating its journey towards sustainability in Great Britain. CCE shares its vision for sustainable manufacturing, offering a picture of what the "factory of the future" may look like in Great Britain by 2050 [26].

• *Canada:* According to the government of Canada, sustainable manufacturing promotes minimizing or eliminating production and processing wastes through eco-efficient practices, and encourages adopting new environmental technologies. Although the manufacturing sector (including primary metal, paper, chemical, and petroleum and coal) significantly contributes greatly to the Canadian economy, the sector has contributed to the inefficient utilization of energy and increased pollution, posing a threat to the environment. The Canadian government is therefore encouraging manufacturing organizations to help fulfill its commitment to reduce the nation's greenhouse gas (GHG) emissions by 20 per cent in the year 2020. Adopting sustainable manufacturing practices can help manufacturing companies reduce their GHG emissions; enhance their brand image; gain a competitive edge; and build trust among the investors, regulators, and customers [27].

• *China:* Chinese manufacturing industry is in a transitional period. Although China is making great developments industrially, there is still a lot of ground to cover. China has launched the Made in China 2025 initiative to bring the Chinese economy to the cutting edge and create a sustainable manufacturing base. By employing AI, China is modernizing their manufacturing and economy. China is also investing in the development of sustainable manufacturing. It will become one of the fastest growing sustainable manufacturing sectors [28].

• *Norway:* Norwegian society is dependent on sustainable value creation. Manufacturing products and services based on the natural factors of our environment should be given priority. A reindustrialization process is also needed so that manufacturing previously outsourced to low-cost countries can return to Norway. The Government's Industry White Paper of March 2017, highlights the need using new materials, digitizing processes, restructuring within sustainable limits, and emphasizing the importance of research and innovation. To attract Norwegian and international players to invest in Norway, it will be necessary to demonstrate that the activity is sustainable [29].

• *India:* A survey of 198 Indian SMEs have identified the following aspects of sustainable manufacturing: "The final quantitative benefits of green manufacturing in order of their decreased ranking are improved morale, improved brand value, lowered regulatory concerns, increased market opportunities, improved product performance, and decreased liabilities. The government has earmarked funds for improving the current infrastructure. Several measures have been taken toward the sensitization on sustainable agricultural methods including optimum use of water and saving as much water as possible for irrigation [30].

7.9 CONCLUSION

Protecting our planet is becoming a priority for everyone. Today, there is a growing awareness of environmental stewardship and sustainability. Sustainability has become an increasingly important requirement for economic activities. It has been applied to many fields such as manufacturing, design, engineering, and environmental stewardship. The implementation of sustainable systems is an essential requirement in modern manufacturing.

A growing number of manufacturers are treating "sustainability" as an important objective in their strategy and operations in order to increase growth and global competitiveness. Sustainable manufacturing, with promising environmental and social benefits, is the wave of the future for manufacturing. It needs to be integral to every aspect of a manufacturer's operations. More information about sustainable manufacturing can be found in the books in [31-55] and the related journals:

- *Sustainability*

- *Manufacturing*

- *International Journal of Sustainable Manufacturing*

- *International Journal of Sustainable Engineering*

- *International Journal of Precision Engineering and Manufacturing-Green Technology*

- *CIRP Journal of Manufacturing Science and Technology*

- *Smart and Sustainable Manufacturing Systems*

REFERENCE

[1]   N. Posinasetti, "Sustainability sustainable manufacturing: Principles, applications and directions," May 2018,

https://www.industr.com/en/sustainable-manufacturing-principles-applications-and-directions-2333598

[2]   M. N. O. Sadiku, U. C. Chukwu. A. Ajayi-Majebi, and S. M. Musa, "Sustainable Manufacturing: A Primer," International Journal of Trend in Scientific Research and Development, vol. 6, no. 5, July-August 2022, pp. 765-769.

[3]   M. N. O. Sadiku, S. R. Nelatury, and S.M. Musa, "Green engineering: A primer," Journal of Scientific and Engineering Research, vol. 5, no.7, 2018, pp. 20-23.

[4]   E. Avramenko, "Contribute to a better world = Be a successful company. Sustainability in a shared-economy startup," February 2018,

https://medium.com/@Anaiska/contribute-to-a-better-world-be-a-successful-company-sustainability-in-a-shared-economy-startup-50cc72f2e37b

[5]   "The three pillars of sustainability,"

https://www.thwink.org/sustain/glossary/ThreePillarsOfSustainability.htm

[6]   M. N. O. Sadiku, O. D. Olaleye, and S. M. Musa, "Sustainable engineering: An introduction," International Journal of Advances in Scientific Research and Engineering, vol. 5, no. 6, June 2019, pp.70-74.

[7]   Athena, "Sustainable development,"

http://macaulay.cuny.edu/eportfolios/akurry/2011/12/21/sustainable-development/

[8]   K. R. Haapalam et al., "Review of engineering research in sustainable manufacturing," Proceedings of the ASME 2011 International Manufacturing Science and Engineering Conference, Corvallis, Oregon, USA, June 13-17, 2011.

[9] H. A. Kishawy, "Sustainable manufacturing and design: Concepts, practices and needs," Sustainability, vol. 4, no. 2, 2012, pp. 154-174.

[10] EPA, "Sustainable manufacturing,"

https://www.epa.gov/sustainability/sustainable-manufacturing#:~:text=Sustainable%20manufacturing%20is%20the%20creation,employee%2C%20community%20and%20product%20safety.

[11] "5 Tips to practice sustainable manufacturing," December 2020,

https://industrytoday.com/5-tips-to-practice-sustainable-manufacturing/

[12] "Sustainable engineering products and manufacturing technologies, 2019," 13th Proceedings of International Symposium on Process Systems Engineering (PSE 2018), 2019.

[13] US Department of Energy, "Chapter 6: Innovating clean energy technologies in advanced manufacturing," July 2015,

https://www.energy.gov/downloads/chapter-6-innovating-clean-energy-technologies-advanced-manufacturing

[14] F. Sanger, "Sustainability tip: Think local first how giving back to your community relates to sustainability," October 2018,

https://blog.walkingmountains.org/sustainability/sustainability-tip-think-local-first-how-giving-back-to-your-community-relates-to-sustainability

[15] G. Appu, "Sustainable manufacturing in automotive industry and how it can be game-changer," March 30, 2021

https://www.financialexpress.com/auto/industry/sustainable-manufacturing-automotive-industry-game-changer-maruti-hyundai-tvs-hero-ashok-leyland/2222895/

[16] D. Basu, A. Misra, and A. J. Puppala, "Sustainability and geotechnical engineering: Perspectives and review," Canadian Geotechnical Journal, vol. 52, 2015, pp. 96-113.

[17] G. Miller, J. Pawloski, and C. R. Standridge, "A case study of lean, usstainable manufacturing," Journal of Industrial Engineering and Management, vol. 3, no. 1, 2010, pp. 11-32.

[18] S. Fotheringham, "Reining in consumption for sustainable manufacturing," "March/April 2018,

https://ispe.org/pharmaceutical-engineering/march-april-2018/reining-consumption-sustainable-manufacturing

[19] "Discover 5 top sustainable manufacturing solutions,"

https://www.startus-insights.com/innovators-guide/discover-5-top-sustainable-manufacturing-solutions/

[20] "How accurate's sustainable manufacturing can benefit your project," June 2019,

https://www.accurateperforating.com/blog/how-accurate%E2%80%99s-sustainable-manufacturing-can-benefit-your-project

[21] E. Raw, " 3 Sustainable manufacturing trends for 2020 and beyond,"

https://www.reliableplant.com/Read/31850/sustainable-manufacturing

[22] K. McAslan, "Reasons to embrace sustainable manufacturing: The new industry standard," May 2018,

https://www.cobizmag.com/reasons-to-embrace-sustainable-manufacturing/

[23] B. Frahm, "Building a sustainable manufacturing enterprise,"

https://www.thefabricator.com/thefabricator/article/shopmanagement/building-a-sustainable-manufacturing-enterprise

[24] S. Rachuri et al. (eds.), "Sustainable manufacturing: Metrics, standards, and infrastructure - NIST Workshop Report," April 2010,

https://www.nist.gov/publications/sustainable-manufacturing-metrics-standards-and-infrastructure-nist-workshop-report

[25] K. C. Morris, "Sustainable manufacturing is smart manufacturing,"

October 2, 2020

https://www.nist.gov/blogs/taking-measure/sustainable-manufacturing-smart-manufacturing

[26]   J. Williamson, "Coca-Cola Enterprises launches vision for sustainable manufacturing," March 2016,

https://www.themanufacturer.com/articles/coca-cola-enterprises-launches-vision-for-sustainable-manufacturing/#:~:text=Coca%2DCola%20Enterprises%20launches%20vision%20for%20sustainable%20manufacturing,-Posted%20on%2022&text=Coca%2DCola%20Enterprises%20(CCE),Sustainable%20Manufacturing%20for%20the%20Future.&text=These%20themes%20set%20the%20agenda%20for%20the%20partnership's%20next%20phase%20of%20research.

[27]   "5 Considerations for employing sustainable manufacturing practices,"

https://www.canadianmetalworking.com/canadianmetalworking/article/management/5-considerations-for-employing-sustainable-manufacturing-practices

[28]   "Sustainability in manufacturing: Made in China 2025 and the BRI," December 2018,

https://et2c.com/sustainability-in-manufacturing/

[29]   "Competitive and sustainable manufacturing,"

https://www.ntnu.edu/iv/competitive-and-sustainable-manufacturing

[30]   "How Indian Fintechs played a pivotal role in enabling Atma Nirbhar Bharat under various domains,"

http://bwsmartcities.businessworld.in/article/How-Indian-Fintechs-Played-A-Pivotal-Role-In-Enabling-Atma-Nirbhar-Bharat-Under-Various-Domains-/30-12-2020-359724/

[31]   G. Seliger, Sustainability in Manufacturing: Recovery of Resources in Product and Material Cycles. Springer Science & Business Media, 2007.

[32]   G. Seliger, (ed.), Sustainable Manufacturing: Shaping Global

Value Creation. Springer, 2012.

[33]   J. Kauffman and K. Mo. Lee, Handbook of Sustainable Engineering. Springer Verlag, 2013.

[34]   A. Pampanelli, N. Trivedi, and P. Found, The Green Factory: Creating Lean and Sustainable Manufacturing. Productivity Press, 2016.

[35]   S. Vinodh, Sustainable Manufacturing: Concepts, Tools, Methods and Case Studies. Boca Raton, FL: CRC Press, 2020.

[36]   J. P. Davim (eds.), Sustainable Manufacturing. Wiley-ISTE, 207.

[37]   S. Vinodh (ed.), Sustainable Manufacturing: Concepts, Tools, Methods and Case Studies. Boca Raton, FL: CRC Press, 2020.

[38]   K. Salonitis and K. Gupta (eds.), Sustainable Manufacturing. Elsevier, 2021.

[39]   G. Seliger, Sustainable Manufacturing: Shaping Global Value Creation. Springer Science & Business Media, 2012.

[40]   W. Li and S. Wang, Sustainable Manufacturing and Remanufacturing Management: Process Planning, Optimization and Applications. Springer, 2018.

[41]   M. Singh, T. Ohji, and R. Asthana, Green and Sustainable Manufacturing of Advanced Material. Elsevier, 2015.

[42]   G. Seliger, M. M. K. Khraisheh, and I. S. Jawahir, Advances in Sustainable Manufacturing. Springer Science & Business Media, 2011.

[43]   K. Gupta, Advanced Manufacturing Technologies: Modern Machining, Advanced Joining, Sustainable Manufacturing. Springer, 2017.

[44]   M. J. Franchetti, B. Elahi, and S. Ghose, Value Creation Through Sustainable Manufacturing. Industrial Press, 2016.

[45]   S. Roberts, Sustainable Manufacturing?:The Case of South Africa and Ekurhuleni. Juta and Company Ltd, 2006.

[46]   A. N. Nambiar and A. H. Sabuwala, Sustainable Manufacturing. Boca Raton, FL: CRC Press, 2014.

[47]   I. Garbie, Sustainability in Manufacturing Enterprises: Concepts, Analyses and Assessments for Industry 4.0. Springer, 2016.

[48]   R. Dubey, Strategic Management of Sustainable Manufacturing Operations. IGI Global, 2016.

[49]   D. Rickerby (ed.), Nanotechnology for Sustainable Manufacturing. Boca Raton, FL: CRC Press, 2014.

[50]   G. Seliger (ed.), Sustainable Manufacturing: Shaping Global Value Creation. Springer 2012.

[51]   N. K. Jha, Green Design and Manufacturing for Sustainability. Boca Raton, FL: CRC Press, 2015.

[52]   K. Kumar, D. Zindani, and J. P. Davim (eds.), Sustainable Engineering Products and Manufacturing Technologies. Academic Press, 2019.

[53]   K. Kumar, D. Zindani, and J. P. Davim (eds.), Sustainable Manufacturing and Design. Woodhead Publishing, 2021.

[54]   K. Jayakrishna et al. (eds.), Sustainable Manufacturing for Industry 4.0: An Augmented Approach. Boca Raton, FL: CRC Press, 2020.

[55]   R. Stark, G. Seliger, and J. Bonvoisin (eds.), Sustainable Manufacturing: Challenges, Solutions and Implementation Perspectives (Sustainable Production, Life Cycle Engineering and Management). Springer, 2017.

CHAPTER 8
SUSTAINABLE AGRICULTURE

"Agriculture is our wisest pursuit because it will in the end contribute most to real wealth, good morals, and happiness."

– Thomas Jefferson

8.1 INTRODUCTION

As depicted in Figure 8.1, every person on earth needs food every day [1]. Modern technology and services have improved the production of food. Agriculture is the largest industry on the planet and it includes crop, horticulture, animal husbandry, forestry, and fisheries. It provides jobs for a significant part of the world population.

Figure 8.1 Every person on earth needs food every day [1].

The world is undergoing changes that will shape the livelihood of millions of people in the coming years. The world's population is expected to grow to about 10 billion by 2050. Meetings the rapidly increasing global food demand with existing farming agricultural practices is likely going to lead to more intense competition for natural resources and land degradation.

Traditional agriculture practices have caused massive deforestation, water scarcities, and soil depletion. It cannot deliver sustainable food and agricultural production. Expanding food production and economic growth using traditional practices have often come at a heavy cost to the natural environment. Therefore, "business-as-usual' is not an option [2].

The sustainable development goals (SDG) of the United Nations are displayed in Figure 8.2 [3].

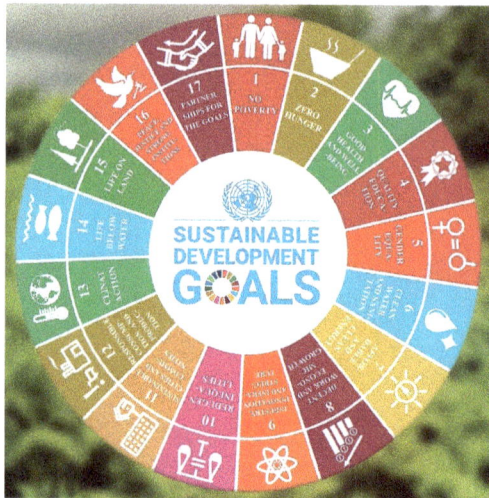

Figure 8.2 The sustainable development goals of the United Nations [3].

For example, SDG 2 aims to end hunger, achieve food security, and improved nutrition, and promote sustainable agriculture. UN has estimated that there will be roughly 10 billion people on earth by the year 2050. Feeding these people has been a major global challenge. The fear that global demand for food will outstrip supply has led to a significant debate. Although farmers have used different means in the past to increase the size of their production, the means that they have used to achieve the growth have reached their limits. Future agriculture will require using new approaches aimed at increasing both productivity and environmental protection. It has been realized that sustainable agriculture is the most realistic way to feed the rapid increasing global population. Sustainable agriculture is one that produces abundant food while protecting the environment and maintaining soil fertility [4,5].

This chapter provides an introduction to sustainable agriculture (SA). It begins with discussing threats to agriculture. It explains sustainable agriculture and some factors affecting it. It addresses campaign for sustainable agriculture. It presents some sustainable agriculture practices. It highlights the benefits and challenges of SA. The last section concludes with comments.

8.2 THREATS TO AGRICULTURE

Farmers face major risks, including extreme weather, long-term climate change, and price volatility in input and product markets, climate change, resource scarcity, and changing consumption patterns. A number of global trends are influencing food security and the overall sustainability of agricultural systems. These include:

- Rapid, global urbanization is accelerating the dietary transition

- Population growth will boost demand for food

- Aging accelerating among rural populations

- The world's farmland is becoming increasingly unsuitable for production

- Climate change will affect every aspect of food production

- Consumers waste 30-40 percent of all food

- Persistent poverty, inequality, and food insecurity

- Hunger is a major problem, particularly in developing countries

- Diverse trends in economic growth, family incomes, agricultural investment, and economic inequality

- Greatly increased competition for natural resources

- Plateauing of agricultural productivity for many crops and animals

- Increased conflicts, crises, and natural disasters

- Structural changes in economic systems and employment implications

- Advanced food production systems and resulting impacts on farmers' livelihoods

- Changes in international financing for sustainable development

- Increasing human demands for food, water, energy, and land has led to a new phenomenon of "land-grabbing."

These issues pose a challenge and are the product of poor foresight and planning. They clearly indicate that agriculture needs innovation, The challenges of tomorrow cannot be resolved with yesterday's methods. We need ways to feed the world population in a sustainable way and in keeping with human dignify. The preservation and sustainable utilization of resources is of vital importance for the interest of all mankind and our environment. Agriculture is at the heart of the sustainability challenge. Interest in sustainable agriculture possibly had its roots in the notion of sustainable development, which is based on intergenerational obligation and equity.

8.3 WHAT IS SUSTAINABLE AGRICULTURE?

Agriculture is one of the biggest threats to a healthy environment. Sustainable agriculture refers to farming that is good for the environment, animals, and people. It is agriculture without depleting the earth's resources or polluting its environment. It may also be regarded as farming in sustainable ways without compromising the ability for current or future generations to meet their needs. It involves farming predicated on the spiritual and practical notions and ethical dimensions of responsible stewardship and sustainable production of wholesome food. It provides a potential solution to enable agricultural systems to feed a growing population without negative effect on the environment and human population. It includes promoting urban farming, which favors equitable access to resources, managed in the most efficient way. A typical example of unsustainable agriculture is the application of fertilizer or manure, which can improve the productivity of a farm but can pollute the environment. An example of growing food in a relatively sustainable way is the practice of growing food in the backyard of houses, schools, etc. [6]. Some of the characteristics of sustainable agriculture are shown in Figure 8.3 [7].

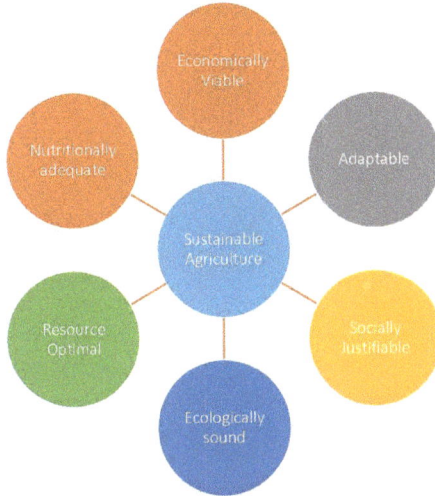

Figure 8.3 Some characteristics of sustainable agriculture [7].

The idea of sustainable agriculture came out of fear and anxiety that the planet's carrying capacity, in terms of the ability to feed humanity, has been reached or even exceeded and the food demand of the rapidly increasing global population cannot be met.

It has become an important topic in international policy due to its potential to reduce environmental risks. The goal of sustainable agriculture is to reduce environmental degradation due to farming. Implementation of sustainable practices in agriculture comes through the adoption environmentally-focused technology.

Sustainability has recently become popular in education, research, and government.

There are three popular definitions of sustainability: sustainability as food sufficiency; sustainability as stewardship; and sustainability as community [8]. As shown in Figure 8.4, practitioners of sustainable agriculture seek to integrate three main objectives into their work: healthy environment, economic profitability, and social and economic equity [9].

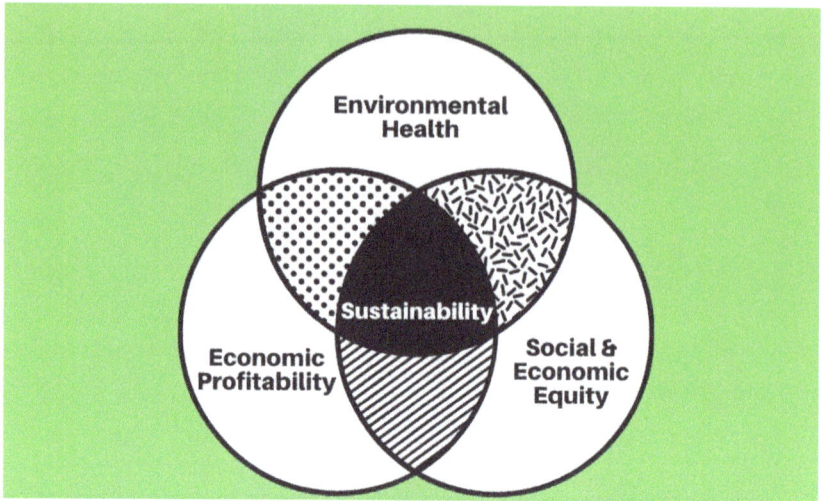

Figure 8.4 Three main objectives of sustainable agriculture [9].

Also, the following items are regarded as the three pillars of sustainability [10]:

• *Profit* over the long term. It uses state-of-the-art, science-based practices that maximize productivity and profit while minimizing environmental damage. Profits exceed the profitability of the conventional system.

• *Stewardship* of our nation's land, air and water. Environmental sustainability in agriculture means good stewardship of the natural systems and resources that farms rely on.

• *Quality* of life for farmers, ranchers, and their communities. Farmer workers should be given the opportunity to form, join a labor union without fear of reprisal, intimidation, or harassment.

The International Institute for Sustainable Development contributes to sustainable development through policy recommendations on economic policy, climate change, natural resources management, and international trade.

As illustrated in Figure 8.5, sustainable agriculture has environmental, social, and economic dimensions considered together [11].

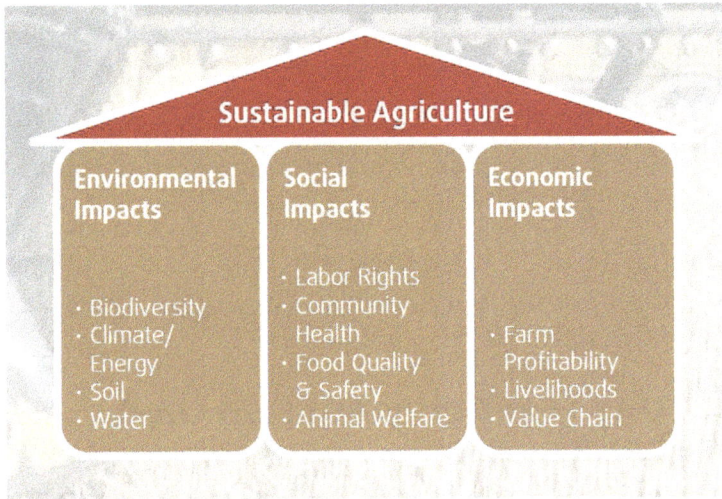

Figure 8.5 Sustainable agriculture has environmental, social, and economic dimensions [11].

Sustainability demands that practices be economically viable, environmentally safe, and socially acceptable. Environmental sustainability promotes agricultural practices that are less dependent on fossil fuels and minimizes their impact on climate change. Social sustainability embraces the capacity of a system to continue to meet society's expectations for social justice and security, including intergenerational equity. Economic sustainability is the capacity for a system to continuously provide goods and services whose values exceed the cost of production [12].

The major characteristics of sustainable agriculture include the following [13]:

- *Conservation and Preservation:* What is taken out of the environment is put back in, so that land and resources such as water, soil and air can be replenished and are available to future generations.

- *Biodiversity:* Farms raise different types of plants and

animals, which are rotated around the fields to enrich the soil and help prevent disease and pest outbreaks. Figure 2 shows cattle in a biodiverse environment [14].

• *Animal Welfare:* Animals are treated humanely and with respect, and are well cared for. They are permitted to carry out their natural behaviors, such as grazing, rooting or pecking.

• *Economically Viable:* Farmers are paid a fair wage and are not dependent on subsidies from the government. Sustainable farmers help strengthen rural communities.

• *Social Justice:* Workers are treated fairly and paid competitive wages and benefits. They work in a safe environment and are offered proper living conditions and food.

8.4 FACTORS AFFECTING SUSTAINABLE AGRICULTURE

The most important factors for a farming site are climate, soil, nutrients and water resources. These factors must be taken into account when addressing sustainable agriculture that can ensure food security for all.

• *Climate Change:* Changing climatic conditions impact yields in a number of different ways depending on crop and location. For example, rising temperatures can cause faster crop development. However, extreme temperatures can damage plant cells and lead to catastrophic losses. Future crop yield changes under climate change [15]. Climate often compels farmers to adapt their agricultural practices. Figure 8.6 shows climate change in America [16].

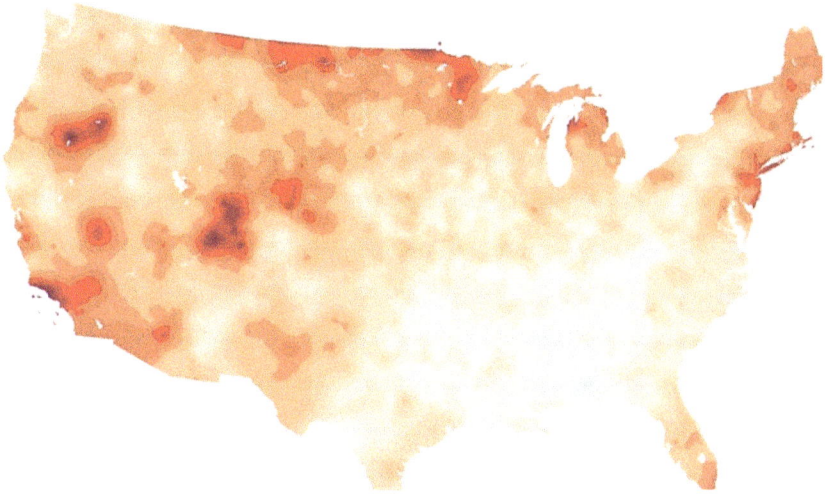

Figure 8.6 Climate change in America [16].

• *Land Areas:* Data on land cover is used to estimate the amount of suitable land available for future farming. Not all regions are suitable for agriculture. Only a small portion of the earth's surface is arable land. Irrigation, plays an important role in enhancing productivity and minimizing the impacts of extreme climate conditions on crop production. Some argue that land reform is an essential step towards reducing social inequalities within the food system. While smallholder farmers in emerging economies may have an opportunity to increase their farm size, farms will remain small in many parts of the developing world [17]. Lands protected by conservation easements provide additional public benefits, including environmental quality and protection of open space.

• *Technology:* Technological advances has introduced radical changes to the agricultural working environment in recent years. For example. smart farming, based on the incorporation of information and communication technologies (ICT) into agricultural production systems, allows a large volume of data to be generated [18]. New technologies are changing the way stakeholders, and government think about the agriculture industry, with the hope for solving the hunger and food scarcity problem. Although technology is certainly part of the solution, it alone cannot solve the global crisis. Some technologies are still expensive to most farmers, especially for the smaller ones and those in developing nations.

8.5 CAMPING FOR SUSTAINABLE AGRICULTURE

Sustainable agriculture requires new approaches to using natural resources and systems. The following areas of consensus have emerged as the key paths of action [19].

1.   Organized small and medium farmers, fully including women farmers, should be a primary focus of investment – recognizing that private enterprise will play a significant role in many solutions

2.   Define the goal in terms of human nutrition rather than simply "more production"

3.   Pursue high yields within a healthy ecology – they are not mutually exclusive and policy and research must reflect that

4.   Impel innovation and the availability of diverse technologies suitable in different socioeconomic and ecological contexts

5.   Significantly reduce waste along the entire food chain

6.   Avoid diverting food crops and productive land for biofuels, but explore decentralized biofuel systems to promote energy and livelihood security that also diversify and restore rural landscapes

7.   Insist on intelligent and transparent measurement of results - we cannot manage what we cannot measure

8.   Develop and adapt public and private institutions that can effectively respond to these new goals

9.   Motivate and reward investments and business systems that result in measurable impacts to the "public good."

10.   Strengthen international and national governance for sustainable resource use, with particular emphasis on the capacity of developing countries to participate

11.   Establish accountability mechanisms for damage to the environment and/or human rights violations and to provide remedies for those rights that are violated.

12.   Produce crops with high yield and nutritional quality to meet

existing and future needs, while keeping resource inputs as low as possible.

13.   Ensure that any adverse effects on soil fertility, water and air quality, and biodiversity from agricultural activities are minimized, and positive contributions are made where possible.

14.   Optimize the use of renewable resources while minimizing the use of non-renewable resources.

8.6 SUSTAINABLE AGRICULTURE PRACTICES

Sustainable agriculture aims to tackle the two main challenges facing humanity resulting from conventional farming practices: environmental degradation and climate change. Through decades of science and practice, the following farming practices have proven effective in achieving sustainability. They are also regarded as the components of sustainable agriculture. They are shown in Figure 8.7 and explained as follows [20]:

Figure 8.7 Components of sustainable agriculture [20].

•   *Crop Rotation:* This means changing the type of crop grown on a particular piece of land from year to year. Planting a variety of crops can have many benefits, including healthier soil and improved pest control. This is a critical feature of sustainable cropping systems because it provides numerous benefits to crop production. It can help conserve, maintain, or replenish soil resources, including organic matter, nitrogen, and other nutrient inputs. It has an important influence on its microbial properties. Unsuitable land management can lead to a loss of soil fertility and a reduction in the abundance and diversity of soil microorganisms. The appropriate choice of crops within the rotation and their sequence is crucial if nutrient cycling within the field system is to be optimized and losses minimized. Crop rotations can increase total soil carbon and nitrogen concentrations over time, which may further improve soil productivity.

- *Intercropping:* This involves cultivating two or more crops in a field simultaneously. It means growing a mix of crops in the same area. It is receiving increasing global interest as an agricultural practice as farmers strive to be more sustainable and maintain soil health. In sustainable agriculture, intercropping plays a major role in the main economic yield balance to farmers and maintains the yield stability of the crops. The positive effects of intercropping include the maintenance of soil water and utilization of the available environmental resources. Therefore, intercropping can lead to improvements in the physiological and biochemical characteristics of the plant rhizosphere, which in turn increases productivity. The beneficial effects of intercropping can also encourage the proliferation of natural enemies, reduce disease and insect injury, and inhibit weed growth all of which undoubtedly lead to positive effects for the final products of the intercropping unit area under sustainable agriculture.

- *Conservation Tillage:* Traditional plowing (tillage) prepares fields for planting and prevents weed problems but can cause soil loss. Using plow and maintaining 30% crop residue on the soil surface after harvest is called conventional tillage practice. In sustainable agricultural production systems, conservation tillage practices have been widely used to alleviate the negative effects of conventional cropland management practices. Typical conservation tillage practices include no-tillage and crop residue retention. No-tillage practices lead to higher carbon and nitrogen concentrations and water content in the surface soil, resulting in increased enzyme. Many conservation tillage systems can improve soil quality over time and reduce the soil erosion risk, improve soil properties, and reduce tillage costs.

- *Green Manuring:* This refers to the practice of incorporating undecomposed green plants into the soil to maintain the nutrient supply to the succeeding crop. It is the process of incorporating green plants into the soil, which are raised in the same field or another field at the green stage before flowering. Today's intensive agricultural practices, crop rotation, and green manuring (GM) offer technology to achieve sustainable production efficiently. One of the options to maintain sustainability in agriculture by restoring soil quality and reclaiming degraded soil is to increase soil organic matter content by green manure crops because this practice is eco-friendly, non-polluting, and non-hazardous to the soil, water, and air. Green manure crops are mainly grown for the benefit of the soil and are very commonly referred to as soil fertility-building crops.

• *Agroforestry:* This is multiple land-use systems in which crops and woody perennials are grown on the same land management unit. Agroforestry system is practiced all over the world, and it has major importance in reducing the impact of climate change. Agroforestry is now receiving increasing attention as a sustainable land management option the world over because of its ecological, economic, and social attributes. Agroforestry offers great promise toward mitigating the rising atmospheric CO_2 levels. The importance of agroforestry cannot be overemphasized, as it has several advantages in the provision of food and other basic needs for a large proportion of the rural population as well as its role in soil fertility restoration and the control of weeds. Advocates have contended that soil conservation is one of its primary benefits. The Association for Temperate Agroforestry defines agroforestry as an intensive land management system that incorporates trees to optimize the benefits they provide when deliberately combined with crops and/or livestock.

8.7 BENEFITS

Sustainable intensification has become a priority for the United Nations. Sustainable agriculture involves using farming techniques that are economically viable, protect the water resources from pollution, treat livestock animals humanely, and maintain soil fertility for future generation. It is a set of principles and practices that aim to eliminate avoidable harm to people, animals, and the environment from food production.

The benefits of sustainable agriculture can be divided into human health benefits and environmental benefits [21]. In terms of human health, crops grown through sustainable agriculture are better for people due to the lack of chemical pesticides and fertilizers. The crops produced through sustainable agriculture can also be more nutritious because the overall crops are healthier and more natural. Sustainable practices lend themselves to smaller, family-scale farms. These farms often find their best niches in local markets, within local food systems, often selling directly to consumers. Other benefits include the following [22-25]:

• *Conserving the Environment:* The goal of sustainable agricultural practices is to decrease environmental degradation due to farming while increasing crop–and thus food–output. SA refers to farming practices that are good for the environment, animals, and people. It has the potential to reduce environmental risks. The reduced reliance on fossil fuels results in the release of less chemicals and pollution into the environment. Sustainable agriculture also benefits the environment by maintaining soil quality, reducing soil degradation and erosion, and saving water. It attempts to minimize the harmful effects on the environment from pollution, wind and water erosion, and other types of environmental damage arising from agricultural production.

• *Reducing Costs:* Moving food from farm to fork in a more efficient manner will benefit everyone involved with the agriculture industry.

• *Standards:* Numerous sustainability standards and certification systems exist. These standards specify rules that producers, manufacturers, and traders need to follow so that the things they make or grow do not hurt people and the environment. These standards are also known as Voluntary Sustainability Standards (VSS) that are private standards that require products to meet specific economic, social or environmental sustainability metrics.

• *Reducing Poverty:* Reducing poverty in rural areas is one of the most sustainable strategies, for which a combination of activities is needed. Sustainable agriculture could be a way to achieve food sovereignty. It could also be a solution to hunger and food security.

A promising proposal to rural poverty reduction within agricultural communities is sustainable economic growth.

• *Saves Energy:* One distinguishing feature of industrial farming is its heavy reliance on energy-intensive machinery, especially fossil fuels. In contrast, sustainable agriculture endeavors to minimize energy use at all levels of production. By eliminating the use of fossil fuels and reducing energy use, sustainable farming helps in reducing greenhouse gas emissions, thereby playing a significant role in combating climate change. The system is designed to recycle a big part of energy on the farm.

• *Stewardship:* Stewardship of both natural and human resources is of prime importance to sustainable agriculture. Stewardship of human resources includes consideration of social responsibilities such as working and living conditions of laborers, the needs of rural communities, and consumer health and safety. Stewardship of natural resources involves maintaining or enhancing this vital resource base for the long term. We must be good custodians of the natural resources.

• *Water Conservation:* Water covers around 71% of the earth's surface. Conventional industrial farming consumes a lot of water to irrigate the vast tracts of land under cultivation. One of the greatest benefits of adopting a sustainable farming approach is the ability to conserve water. Efficient irrigation systems, careful measuring of water use, recycling water, capturing rainwater, and treating grey water are just a few of the activities sustainable farmers do to improve their use of earth's most precious resource.

• *Reduces Waste:* Sustainable farming uses natural inputs to fertilize crops and keep pests at bay. In most farms, even the waste is re-integrated into the ecosystem and does not pollute the environment.

• *Promotes Soil Health:* Sustainable farms often use methods such as crop rotation and polycultures to help promote soil health. By rotating crops, nutrient levels in the soil are given time to replenish.

• *Public Health:* Sustainable agriculture offers solutions for the negative health consequences of the industrial food system. In search of short-term profit, corporations prioritize higher yields, outward appearance, and shelf life over nutrition for optimal health. Sustainable agriculture, on the other hand, aims to grow fresh and nutritious foods for local food webs, for example, by improving soil health. Managing soil health and nutrient cycling are important prerequisites for ensuring the presence of optimal levels of healthful vitamins and minerals in harvested crops.

• *Energy Efficiency:* Sustainable farming often relies on the use of renewable resources to power and manage the farm. Running rivers also provide a source of hydroelectric power.

• *Economic Opportunities:* Sustainable farming can provide additional economic opportunities, for both the farm and employees. Using natural methods can also mean more work available for workers.

• *Animal Welfare:* Sustainable agriculture practices can help to decrease the intensity of animal farming, allowing animals to live more autonomously in smaller numbers in healthy natural environments.

• *Food:* Sustainable agriculture is based on principles that aim at improving the livelihoods of rural populations by empowering small farmers to grow locally-sourced food. Its aim is that the food is grown in the area, using local resources to feed local people, which is the most direct and the least wasteful way of managing diminishing resources. The localized approach encourages respect for the land and responsible management of resources.

• *Food Security:* This can be achieved through the conservation of natural resources for sustainable agriculture. These resources are soil, water, energy, and air, and their availability for crop production in the future essentially depends on their correct management today.

Figure 8.8 depicts some of the benefits of sustainable agriculture.

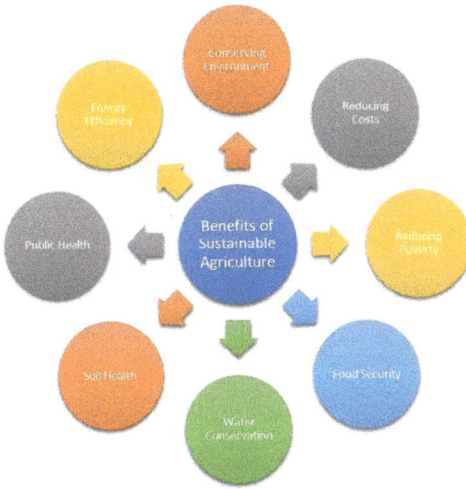

Figure 8.8 Benefits of sustainable agriculture.

8.8 CHALLENGES

The challenges facing agriculture over the coming decades are many and complex. The barriers to sustainable agriculture can be broken down and understood through three different dimensions. These three dimensions are seen as the core pillars to sustainability: social, environmental, and economic pillars. While significant progress has been made towards achieving the sustainable development goals, critical environmental, social, economic and institutional challenges are still to be overcome. Two crucial connected challenges are [26]: (1) the persistently high levels of hunger and malnutrition – particularly in the rural areas of many developing countries – only slowly declining rates of poverty; and (2) an unsustainable and increasing burden of human activities on the earth's carrying capacity. Some researchers affirm that food insecurity, hunger, and poverty are not technical issues caused by insufficient food production, but rather political issues related to uneven distribution. Lack of governmental initiatives, research, and material base for site-specific applications are among the challenges that may arise. Other challenges of sustainable agriculture include the following:

• *Complexity:* Sustainable agriculture is a very complex concept and it means different things for different people. Farms are ecologically complex, benefiting from natural processes such as soil microbe activity, rainwater availability, and pollination by insects or wind. It is difficult, if not impossible, to accurately assess the exact monetary value of the many ecological aspects of farming.

• *Complex Decision Making:* Managing the decision-making processes of farming has always been complex because there are so many different limiting factors that are not within a farmer's control. The weather itself being chief among them. Data-driven weather intelligence is the key to sustainability.

• *Doing More for Less:* The amount of arable land remains constant. As the population steadily grows, we will need to produce more crops from existing resources.

• *Different Concepts of Sustainability:* Defining agricultural sustainability, as with every other sustainability concept, is a challenging task. Sustainable agriculture means many things to different people in agriculture. At least three different definitions of sustainability are available: sustainability as food sufficiency; sustainability as stewardship; and sustainability as community. Agricultural researchers and policy makers should integrate these various views of sustainability [27].

• *Global Agriculture:* This is often blamed for many of the pressing social and environmental challenges facing us today, such as climate change. Although global agriculture is part of the problem of climate change, it is also part of the solution. The climate crisis is affecting everyone, not least of all farmers. They are at the forefront of changing weather systems and bear the brunt of the extremes of our climate and markets.

8.9 CONCLUSION

Agriculture is essential to international development. Sustainable agriculture is a kind of agriculture that focuses on producing long-term crops and livestock while having minimal effects on the environment. It produces abundant food without depleting the earth's resources or polluting its environment. Its goal is to meet society's food and textile needs in the present without compromising the ability of future generations to meet their own needs. It is an agricultural production that is economically viable and does not degrade the environment over the long run. Proper protection, management, and governance of the environment are therefore crucial to sustainable agriculture.

Sustainable agriculture is the need of time. In the field of agriculture, sustainability helps to seek out the right balance between the need for food production and preservation of environmental ecosystems. More information about sustainable agriculture can be found in the books in [28-63] and the following related journals:

- *The Journey to Sustainability Begins With Education*

- *Sustainability, American Journal of Alternative Agriculture*

- *Journal of Sustainable Agriculture and Environment*

- *Journal of Agriculture Environment & Food Security*

REFERENCE

[1]   "Sustainable agriculture vs. industrial agriculture," April 2023,
https://foodprint.org/issues/sustainable-agriculture-vs-industrial-agriculture/#:~:text=Industrialized%20agriculture%20is%20highly%20concentrated,animal%20welfare%2C%20is%20g-aining%20traction.

[2]   FAO, The future of food and agriculture: Trends and challenges. Rome, Food and Agriculture Organization of the United Nations. 2017.

[3]   "Natural farming for sustainable development goals,"
https://naturalfarming.niti.gov.in/sustainable-development-goals/#:~:text=Natural%20Farming%20for%20Sustainable%20Development%20Goals,-Agroecological%20practices%20like&text=This%20method%20would%20ensure%20food,generating%20crops%20throughout%20the%20year.

[4]   M. N. O. Sadiku, P. O. Adebo, A. Ajayi-Majebi, and S. M. Musa, "Sustainable agriculture," International Journal of Engineering Research & Technology, vol. 10, no. 9, September 2021, pp. 353-358.

[5]   M. N. O. Sadiku, U. C. Chukwu, Adeniyi Ogunnusi, and S. M. Musa, "Environmental Sustainability: A primer," International Journal of Trend in Scientific Research and Development, vol. 6, no. 4, June 2022, pp. 369-375.

[6]   "What is sustainable agriculture?" Sustainable Agriculture Research and Education (SARE),
https://www.sare.org/resources/what-is-sustainable-agriculture/

[7]   https://www.researchgate.net/figure/Characteristics-of-Sustainable-Agriculture_fig1_341043740

[8]   "Sustainable agriculture," Wikipedia, the free encyclopedia https://en.wikipedia.org/wiki/Sustainable_agriculture

[9]   M. Denton, "What is sustainable agriculture?" September 2020,

https://www.postharvest.com/blog/what-is-sustainable-agriculture/

[10]   R. Lowrance, P. F. Hendrix, and E. P. Odum, "A hierarchical approach to sustainable agriculture," American Journal of Alternative Agriculture, November 2009.

[11]   "A short guide to sustainable agriculture,"

https://sustainablefoodlab.org/a-short-guide-to-sustainable-agriculture/

[12]   G. P. Robertson, "A sustainable agriculture?" Dædalus, the Journal of the American Academy of Arts & Sciences, vol.144, no. 4, Fall 2015, pp.76-89.

[13]   "What is sustainable agriculture?"

https://www.cbf.org/join-us/more-things-you-can-do/buy-fresh-buy-local/what-is-sustainable-agriculture.html

[14]   "Sustainable agriculture: A short report by compassion in world farming 2008,"

https://www.ciwf.org.uk/media/3817786/sustainable-agriculture-report.pdf

[15]   FAO, The future of food and agriculture: Alternative pathways to 2050. Rome, Food and Agriculture Organization of the United Nations. 2018.

[16]   S.   Mufson   et   al.,   "2°C: beyond   the   limit: Extreme climate change has arrived in America,"

https://www.washingtonpost.com/graphics/2019/national/climate-environment/climate-change-america/

[17] Oxfam, "the future of agriculture: synthesis of an online debate," July 2013,

https://oi-files-d8-prod.s3.eu-west-2.amazonaws.com/s3fs-public/file_attachments/dp-future-of-agriculture-synthesis-300713-en_0_0.pdf

[18] A. Trivedi1 and N. Nandeha, "Smart farming: The future of agriculture," Agriculture & Food: E-Newsletter, October 2020.

[19] D. Giovannucci et al., "Food and Agriculture: the future of sustainability,"

United Nations Department of Economic and Social Affairs Division for Sustainable Development, March 2012,

https://sustainabledevelopment.un.org/content/documents/1443sd21brief.pdf

[20] J. Suman et al., "Microbiome as a key player in sustainable agriculture and human health,"

https://www.frontiersin.org/articles/10.3389/fsoil.2022.821589/full

[21] "What is sustainable agriculture?"

https://study.com/academy/lesson/what-is-sustainable-agriculture-definition-benefits-and-issues.html

[22] J. Ciempa, "The benefits of sustainable agriculture and how we get there," March 2021,

https://www.ibm.com/blog/the-benefits-of-sustainable-agriculture-and-how-we-get-there/

[23]   "What is sustainable ag?"

https://sustainableagriculture.net/about-us/what-is-sustainable-ag/

[24]   "The benefits of sustainable farming," November 2021,

https://www.jerseygirlorganics.co.nz/post/the-benefits-of-sustainable-farming

[25]   "The triple bottom line of sustainable agriculture,"

https://www.farmlandlp.com/2009/11/triple-bottom-line-sustainable-agriculture/#.YTKpK45KguU

[26]   "TST issues brief: Sustainable agriculture,"

https://sustainabledevelopment.un.org/content/documents/1802tstissuesagriculture.pdf

[27] R. Lowrance, P. F. Hendrix, and E. P. Odum, A hierarchical approach to sustainable agriculture," November 2009,

https://www.cambridge.org/core/journals/american-journal-of-alternative-agriculture/article/abs/hierarchical-approach-to-sustainable-agriculture/0BDB17477E5D48DF5CF186FE0E740986

[28]   C. Sachs et al., The Rise of Women Farmers and Sustainable Agriculture. University of Iowa Press; 2016.

[29]   Z. A. Siddiqui and K. Futai (eds.), Mycorrhizae: Sustainable Agriculture And Forestry. Dordrecht: Springer, 2008.

[30]   C. A. Edwards, Sustainable Agricultural Systems. CRC Press, 2020.

[31]   I. F. García-Tejero et al., Water and Sustainable Agriculture. Springer Netherlands, 2011.

[32]   R. L. Ison, Teaching Threatens Sustainable Agriculture. London, UK: Sustainable Agriculture Programme of the International Institute for Environment and Development, 1990.

[33]   M. A. Altieri, Agroecology: The Science Of Sustainable Agriculture. CRC Press, 2018.

[34]   J. F. Power and R. Prasad, Soil Fertility Management For Sustainable Agriculture. CRC press, 1997.

[35]   F. J. Villalobos and E. Fereres (eds.), Principles of agronomy for sustainable agriculture. New York, NY: Springer, 2016.

[36]   A. N. Yadav et al. (eds.), Agriculturally important fungi for sustainable agriculture. Cham: Springer, 2020.

[37]   S. R. Gliessman and M. Rosemeyer (eds.), The Conversion To Sustainable Agriculture: Principles, Processes, and Practices. CRC Press, 2009.

[38]   C. A. Francis, C. B. Flora, and L. D. King (eds.), Sustainable agriculture in temperate zones. John Wiley & Sons, 1991.

[39]   J. Singh and A. N. Yadav (eds.), Natural bioactive products in sustainable agriculture. Springer Nature, 2020.

[40]   C. H. Burton and C. Turner, Manure management: Treatment strategies for sustainable agriculture. Editions Quae, 2003.

[41]   National Research Council, Sustainable Agriculture and The Environment in The Humid Tropics. National Academies Press, 1993.

[42]   R. P. Poincelot (ed.), Toward a More Sustainable Agriculture. Springer Science & Business Media, 2012.

[43]   S. R. Gliessman, E. Engles, and R. Krieger, Agroecology: Ecological Processes in Sustainable Agriculture. CRC press, 1998.

[44]   T. Satyanarayana, B. N. Johri, and A. Prakash (eds.), Microorganisms in Sustainable Agriculture and Biotechnology. Springer Science & Business Media, 2012.

[45]   T. Higa and J. F. Parr, Beneficial and Effective Microorganisms for a Sustainable Agriculture and Environment. Atami: International Nature Farming Research Center, 1994.

[46]   F. Magdoff and R. R. Weil (eds.), Soil Organic Matter in Sustainable Agriculture. CRC press, 2004.

[47]   M. K. Jhariya et al.(eds.), Sustainable Agriculture, Forest and Environmental Management. Springer, 2019.

[48]   N. Hassanein, Changing the Way America Farms: Knowledge and Community in The Sustainable Agriculture Movement. University of Nebraska Press, 1999.

[49]   National Research Council, Toward Sustainable Agricultural Systems in the 21st Century. National Academies Press, 2010.

[50]   J. L. Caviglia, Sustainable agriculture in Brazil. Edward Elgar, 1999.

[51]   J.M. Antle and S. Ray, Sustainable Agricultural Development: An Economic Perspective. Springer, 2020.

[52]   M. Farooq, N. Gogoi, and M. Pisante (e4ds.), Sustainable Agriculture and the Environment. Elsevier, 2023.

[53]   N. Mandal, A. Dey, and R. Rakshit, Soil Management for Sustainable Agriculture: New Research and Strategies. Apple Academic Press, 2022.

[54]   A. Singh et al., Nanopriming: Approach to Sustainable Agriculture. IGI Global, 2023.

[55]   S. R. Gliessman and M. Rosemeyer (eds.), The Conversion to Sustainable Agriculture: Principles, Processes, and Practices. Boca Raton:FL: CRC Press, 2009.

[56]   J. L. Hatfield and L. K. Douglas, Sustainable Agriculture Systems. CRC Press, 1993.

[57]   A. N. Yadav, Plant Microbiomes for Sustainable Agriculture: Current Research and Future Challenges. Springer International Publishing, 2020.

[58]   N. K. Arora, S. Mehnaz, and R. Balestrini (eds.), Bioformulations: For Sustainable Agriculture. Berlin: Springer, 2016.

[59]   D. K. Verma (ed.), Microbiology for Sustainable Agriculture, Soil Health, and Environmental Protection. Apple Academic Press, 2021.

[60]   K. Boole et al. (eds.), Advances in Crop Modelling for a Sustainable Agriculture. Burleigh Dodds Science Publishing, 2019.

[61]   E. Lichtfouse (ed.), Sustainable Agriculture Reviews. Springer 2017.

[62]   J. Mason, Sustainable Agriculture. Landlinks Press, 2003.

[63]   E. Lighthouse et al. (eds.), Sustainable Agriculture. Dordrecht: Springer Netherlands, 2009.

CHAPTER 9
SUSTAINABLE ENERGY

"Energy is essential for development, and sustainable
energy is essential for sustainable development."

– Tim Wirth

9.1 INTRODUCTION

It is well known that all processes in the universe are energy driven. It is also a fact that energy can neither be created nor destroyed but can only be transformed from one form to another. There are various types of energy: electrical energy, chemical energy, nuclear energy, thermal energy, gravitational energy, potential energy, etc. Energy is crucially important in the economic and social development of any society. The use of energy is evident in our everyday lives. We need energy in lighting, heating, cooling, transport, communication, systems, domestic appliances, and battery-powered devices to mention but a few. The socio-economic growth of any nation cannot materialize until there is a significant improvement in the energy supply in the country. The conventional type of energy is fossil-based energy, which generally includes coal, petroleum, natural gas, etc. Energy that comes from these conventional means is called "brown energy." Another type of energy is "green energy," which is clean source of energy with a lower environmental impact compared to conventional sources [1,2].

Green energy, which is sometimes called renewable or sustainable energy, comes from natural sources like wind, water, and sunlight. It is often called "clean" because it produces no pollutants. It is an attractive option because it provides a clean and earth-friendly alternative to traditional energy. It is illustrated in Figure 9.1 [3].

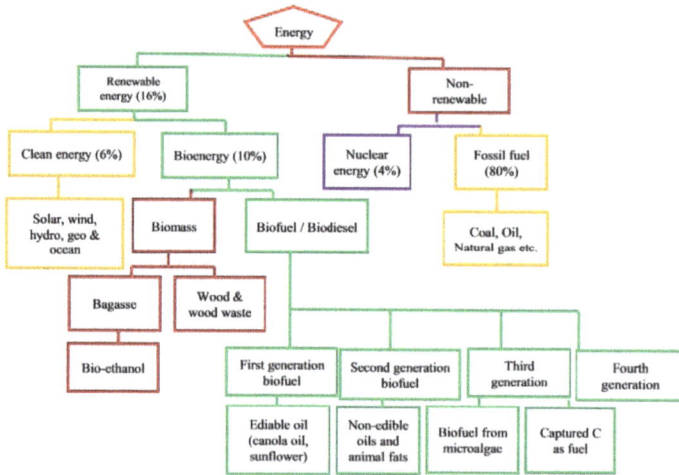

Figure 9.1 Green sources [3].

As Sherrod Brown (a US senator) rightly said, "Green energy is an environmental strategy, a national security strategy, an economic strategy. Investing in its development and production is both right and smart. Failing to invest in it is a risk to the future of our nation and our planet" [4].

Solving the energy crisis is one of the most essential undertakings of the 21st century. Concerns about climate change and global warming are driving increasing sustainable energy legislation. Energy becomes sustainable if it meets the needs of the present without compromising the ability of future generations to meet their own needs. Sustainable energy is a form of energy that does not contribute to climate change or global warming. It uses energy sources that are continually replenished by nature. It can fulfill the need for energy while saving the planet.

This chapter briefly reviews major types of sustainable energy and their usage. It begins by presenting the conventional or brown energy. It explains the concepts of sustainability and sustainable energy. It covers different types of sustainable energy sources. It presents some uses or applications of sustainable energy. It addresses the benefits and challenges of sustainable energy. The last section concludes the chapter.

9.2 CONVENTIONAL ENERGY

Energy may be defined as the capacity to do work. Energy resources help in creating wealth and improving living standards. The availability and affordability of energy sources are crucial for the overall economic development of a nation. Conventional sources of energy are from non-renewable fossil fuels (coal, oil, gas, petroleum, etc.) and nuclear power [5]. Fossil fuels have been used as a common source of energy for centuries. Petroleum springs and coal mines are not inexhaustible but are rapidly diminishing in many places. A lot of attention has focused on the environmental impacts of conventional energy sources, particularly fossil fuels.

Energy that comes from these conventional means is called "brown" (carbon-intensive) energy. Grid power is a mixture of brown and renewable energies. It is regarded as a kind of brown energy source because utilities produce much of their power by burning carbon-intensive fossil fuels, such as coal and natural gas. Most brown energy sources (such as fossil fuel power, gas turbine, coal, and oil) are able to adjust their output power on demand through tuning the power generator. If brown energy must be used, the scheduler selects times when it is cheap.

The brown energy system contributes to many environmental problems, including climate change, air pollution, biodiversity loss, the release of toxins into the environment, and water scarcity. As of 2019, 85% of the world's energy needs are met by burning fossil fuels. The burning of fossil fuels and biomass is a major source of air pollution, which causes untimely deaths. To reduce the harmful effects of brown energy, sustainable energy sources need to be applied. Although each country has both traditional power plants and sustainable energy plants, there is a need for a change in the energy consumption pattern. Meeting existing and future energy demands in a sustainable way is a critical challenge for the global goal of limiting climate change. Earth resources are limited and are increasingly depleting. This compels governments and environmental activists all over the world to emphasize the need to switch from conventional resources to alternative green sources [6]. Sustainable energy is the type that produces few externalities for environment. It uses electricity and gas made from renewable sources. As the costs of brown or non-renewable energy grow, renewable energy becomes more widely used.

9.3 CONCEPT OF SUSTAINABILITY

Sustainability simply means the ability to maintain or support a process continuously over time. It refers to meeting the needs of the present without compromising the ability of future generations to meet their own needs. However, in business and policy contexts, sustainability seeks to prevent the depletion of natural or physical resources, so as to remain available for the long term. The three pillars of sustainability are economic, environmental, and social – also informally known as profits, planet, and people (the 3Ps).

Sustainable energy is a significant aspect of sustainability, an important consideration for human development and activity. Entrenchment of energy efficiency and conservation is very much needed as a practical strategy to reduce energy demand. Goal number 7 of the United Nations' Sustainable Development Goals (SDGs) requires that by 2030 all nations should:

a. Ensure universal access to affordable and reliable modern energy services

b. Substantially increase the share of renewable energy in the global energy mix

c. Double the rate of improvement of energy efficiency.

Sustainable development is not achievable without sustainable energy. Energy can be a powerful tool for sustainable development, which should meet the needs of the present without compromising the ability of future generations to meet their own needs. The goal is to minimize the damage we humans inflict on the planet; the damage will never be eliminated. Redirecting energy to work towards that goal will require major policy changes within the overall enabling framework. Policies can support sustainable development by [7]:

•	Delivering adequate and affordable energy supplies—including liquid and gaseous fuels for cooking and electricity for domestic and commercial use—to unserved areas.

•	Encouraging energy efficiency.

- Accelerating the use of new renewables.

- Widening the diffusion and use of other advanced energy technologies.

9.4 SUSTAINABLE ENERGY

Sustainable energy is energy that is capable of meeting the energy needs of the present without compromising the resources and energy supply of the future. It is the key to the transition to a new energy model, capable of addressing three global challenges: environmental conservation, energy security, and socio-economic development. The concept of "sustainable energy" was brought to the global fore few years ago and since then it has gained prominence. This was as a result of climate change brought about by environmental pollution, caused by man's reckless exploitation of natural resources and release of harmful wastes, leading to global warming, greenhouse gas emissions, etc.

Sustainable energy is the urgent solution required to save the environment and combat global warming. The working definitions of sustainable energy encompass multiple dimensions of sustainability such as environmental, economic, and social dimensions. Energy sources with low environmental impact are called green energy or clean energy. The economic dimension of sustainability covers economic development, efficient use of energy, and energy security to ensure that each country has constant access to sufficient energy. Sustainable energy such as wind and solar energy creates zero carbon emissions that can harm the atmosphere and contribute to global warming [8]. As Phil Harding rightly said,

Sustainable energy + food security + healthy environment = full employment + better future.

"Renewable energy" and "sustainable energy" are often used interchangeably. There is some overlap between the two, as many sustainable energy sources are also renewable. Although both sustainable energy and renewable energy are critical to the future of our planet, there are subtle distinctions between the two forms of energy. Not all renewable energy is sustainable, and not all sustainable energy sources are renewable. Renewable energy refers to those types of energy that use non-finite resources. It is usable energy created through naturally recurrent processes. Some common examples of renewable energy sources are solar, wind, hydro, tidal, geothermal, and biomass. Excessive use of renewable resources can render a particular energysource unsustainable. Some renewable energy sources, like biomass, are not strictly sustainable. Energy is "sustainable" when it can meet a company or a society's needs without being depleted or becoming unusable in some fashion. Sustainable energy is an energy resource that can be maintained for the foreseeable future without compromising or threatening future generations. How energy is created, distributed, and consumed are the key factors in determining whether or not a given energy source is sustainable [9]. The most popular sources of sustainable energy, including wind, solar, and hydropower, are also renewable.

9.5 TYPES OF SUSTAINABLE ENERGY

Sustainable energy is regarded as a form of energy that can be utilized again and again without putting a source in danger of getting depleted. It is generated from sources such as solar, wind, geothermal, and biomass. There are different forms of green energy depending on the sources [10,11]. The sun plays a crucial role in most types of renewable energy since they depend on it one way or the other.

• *Solar:* This involves capturing the sun's energy with photovoltaic (PV) cells. The solar cells absorb the solar radiation from the sun and convert the energy into direct current electricity. This energy can be collected and converted in different ways. It can be harnessed through a range of technologies like solar heating and photovoltaic. Solar energy generation depends on various factors such as the temperature, the solar intensity, and the geolocation of the solar panels. Solar energy is the fastest growing renewable, while solar photovoltaics is the largest renewable employer. For example, a building can be constructed to incorporate a solar hot water, cooling or ventilation system. Solar energy can supply solar heat to houses and industrial processes. Figure 9.2 shows a solar farm outside Orlando, Florida, USA [12].

Figure 9.2 A solar farm outside [12].

•   *Wind:* Wind energy is produced by wind turbines with rotating blades capturing the wind flow and harnessing the wind's kinetic energy to generate electricity. It requires extensive area coverage to produce significant amounts of energy. For example, wind turbines may be used to generate electricity as a supplement to an company's existing power supply. Wind is most likely the safest form of green energy in terms of its overall ecological impacts. Wind energy is the most advanced renewable energy. Figure 9.3 displays a wind turbine and how it works [13]. A wind turbine converts kinetic energy from the wind into electricity.

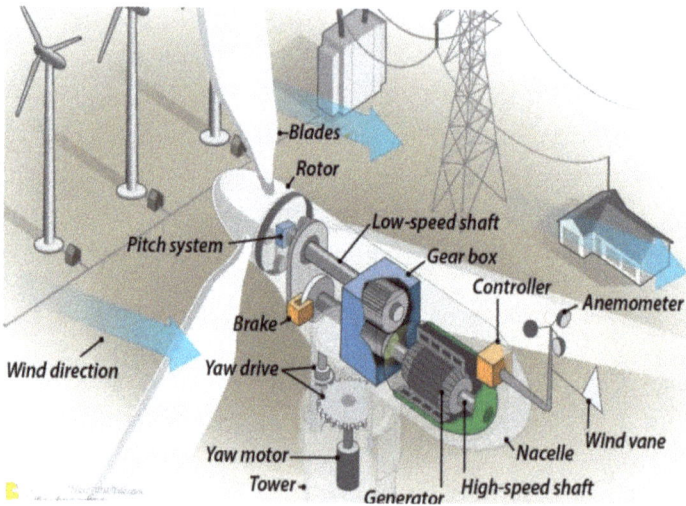

Figure 9.3 A wind turbine and how it works [13].

- *Hydroelectric:* Hydropower ranks among the energy sources with the lowest levels of greenhouse gas emissions. It is the largest source of renewable electricity, while solar and wind energy are growing rapidly. As shown in Figure 9.4, moving water is responsible for powering turbines and generating hydroelectric power [14]. The turbines are connected to generators which harness the mechanical energy from the water currents and convert it into hydroelectricity. This is often regarded as the largest source of renewable energy because it provides more than 97% of all electricity generated by renewable sources worldwide. Strictly speaking, hydropower is not renewable because it has the largest environmental impacts partly due to the need to construct dams which block animal migration and disrupt river flows. For example, small towns can harness the energy of local rivers by building hydroelectric power systems.

Figure 9.4 Moving water is responsible for generating hydroelectric power [14].

•   *Geothermal Energy:* As the name implies, geothermal energy is heat energy from the earth itself. The temperature of the earth steadily increases with depth. Geothermal power plants harness the heat sources to produce electricity, which is cost effective, reliable, sustainable, and non-polluting or eco-friendly. A major challenge with this energy source is that plants are expensive to build. For example, geothermal energy may be used for heating/cooling office buildings or manufacturing plants. Unlike solar and wind, which are intermittent, geothermal energy can be generated 24/7. Figure 9.5 depicts a geothermal power plant in Salton Sea, California, USA [12].

Figure 9.5 A geothermal power plant [12].

• *Biomass:* This is renewable organic material that comes from plants and animals. It is produced when organic wastes decay. This waste can be converted to fuel through combustion for the generation of electricity. Biomass is mankind's original source of energy. The most popular form is burning trees for cooking and warmth. Geothermal and biomass power plants may require water for cooling. For example, farm operations can convert waste from livestock into electricity. Unlike solar and wind, biomass power is dispatchable, i.e. it can be turned on and off.

• *Ocean Energy:* This is also referred to as marine energy. It refers to the source of energy carried by ocean waves, tides, and temperature differences in oceans. The movement of water in the oceans creates a vast store of kinetic energy, which can be harnessed to generate electricity to power homes and industries.

These are produced with the same goal in mind, which is to save the planet. Some of these renewable and sustainable energy can be harnessed to generate electricity. Countries such as Iceland and Norway have reached 100% renewable energy generation, i.e. all their electricity is generated using renewable energy. Renewable energy technologies are getting cheaper due to mass production and market competition.

9.6 APPLICATIONS

Rapid advances in sustainable energy technologies are improving the efficiency of generating electricity using renewable sources, and also driving down the cost of deploying a power system. Here we present some usages or applications of sustainable energy.

• *Smart Home:* Home energy consumption, such as electricity, heating, and cooling, has been an important environmental and economic issue for decades. Constraints such as renting, safety, and unsupportive household members affect energy use and energy saving behaviours of customers [15]. A smart home provides optimum living conditions required naturally. Green renewable energy source (such as solar panel) has been utilized in generating power for all the smart appliances used to sustain the smart home. Solar heat energy has been used to generate hot water and do the cooking. Using the sustainable energy source in smart home can reduce energy cost and minimize wastage of energy [16]. A typical solar energy generation at home is shown in Figure 9.6 [17].

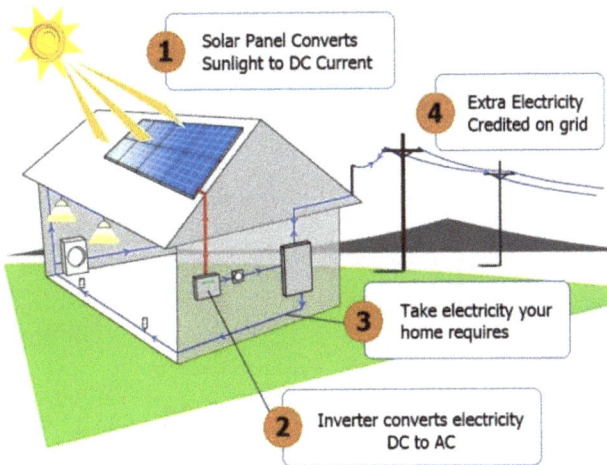

Figure 9.6 A typical example of solar energy generation in a home [17]

• *Businesses:* Reducing energy usage is not limited to household. For businesses, it is important to effectively reduce electricity consumption and environmental pollution. Switching to sustainable energy can actually bring many different benefits to a business. The benefits include lower energy bills, boosting public relations, creating jobs, and great return on investment [18].

• *Data Centers:* Data centers are known for consuming an enormous amount of electricity. Mega data centers (such as those of Apple, Microsoft, and Google) have emerged due to the soaring demand for IT services. Data center operators are constantly under pressure to minimize the carbon footprint. To achieve this requires powering data centers by on-site generation of renewable energy. Renewable energy integration lowers the cost of designing fault tolerant distributed data centers with reduced carbon footprint. To reduce costs and environmental impacts, modern datacenters operators, such as those of Google and Apple, are beginning to integrate renewable energy sources into their power supply [19,20]. A typical datacenter is illustrated in Figure 9.7 [21].

Figure 9.7 A typical datacenter [21].

• *Mobile Networks:* These are among the major energy guzzlers. The growing energy consumption leads to a significant rise of carbon footprints. Therefore, greening mobile networks is becoming a necessity for economic and environmental sustainability. Sustainable energy is a promising energy alternative for future mobile networks [22].

• *Cellular Networks:* The increase in a number of mobile

users and their diverse data applications is compelling cellular network operators to install more base stations (BSs). Concerns about increasing number of BSs with high energy consumption have prompted cellular operators to deploy renewable energy sources in BSs. This helps reduce the on-grid consumption and operational expenditure. Powering cellular networks with renewable energy sources is a promising alternative for reducing global carbon footprint [23].

• *Electric Vehicles:* The advent of electric vehicles has created a new paradigm shift on oil and gas in the world as a whole. This is because several nations have already decided that in the next 20-30 years oil-based transport fuels, that currently constitute 60-70% of their oil and gas consumptions, will be replaced by electric vehicles. The technical capabilities of electric cars are taking great strides, and the popularity of these vehicles is also growing among consumers. Since most of America's electricity still comes from fossil fuels, electric vehicles charged by that source of energy indirectly generate greenhouse gasses. But as our sources of electricity transition from fossil fuels, the infrastructure of electric vehicles and charging stations will be in place and will facilitate the reduction of greenhouse gases. The critical element will be the development of sustainable energy that is inexpensive and reliable.

Other applications include sustainable-energy buildings, cognitive radio networks, cyber–physical systems, and for battlefield.

9.7 BENEFITS

Sustainable energy comes from renewable sources and its production process does not generate an environmental impact. It offers a number of benefits to businesses and institutions. Choosing sustainable energy is a prudent step towards more sustainable operations and practices and a demonstration of environmental stewardship. The renewable energy industry is more labor intensive and supports thousands of jobs. It is providing stable and affordable electricity. Sustainable energy is, both in its source and in its production process, clean and environmentally friendly. It plays a key role in decarbonizing the energy supply. Countries may support renewables to create jobs. Governments can make the transition to sustainable energy more politically and socially feasible. Many homeowners can sell excess solar or wind energy to their utility companies. This way, they can pay off their energy investments quickly. Other benefits of sustainable energy include [24-27].

1. *Energy Efficiency:* This involves using less energy to deliver the same goods or services. It is a cornerstone of many sustainable energy strategies. The International Energy Agency (IEA) has estimated that increasing energy efficiency could achieve 40% of greenhouse gas emission reductions. Improving energy efficiency at homes, businesses, offices, schools, governments, and industries is cost-effective way to address the challenges of high energy prices and energy. Sometimes energy efficiency may mean changing behaviors, such as drying clothes on a clothesline instead of a dryer. Better ways to produce solar photovoltaic panels are lowering panel production cost. Governments can promote energy efficiency by setting energy efficiency standards. Products that meet high-efficiency standards should receive the Energy Star label. Efficiency labels inform consumers about the energy efficiency of different products. Unfortunately, even with informative labels, some consumers do not purchase high-efficiency products because the upfront costs may be higher than regular.

2. *Energy Conservation:* Energy can be conserved by increasing the technical efficiency of appliances, vehicles, industrial processes, and buildings. The transition to sustainable energy sources minimizes dependence on large quantities of water, which helps conserve water resources and prevent water scarcity.

3. *Energy Security:* The concept of energy security implies that energy supply must be capable of supplying all people and sectors of activity, and that it must be carried out in a sustainable way. This is securing energy supply and ensuring that this is done in an economically and environmentally sustainable manner. This has become a priority for all countries.

4. *Growth:* Sustainable energy provides new opportunities for growth. It enables businesses to grow, generates jobs, and creates new markets. Nations can grow more resilient, competitive economies. With sustainable energy, they can build the clean energy economies of

the future.

5.   *Prosperity:* Sustainable energy has the potential to lift the poorest nations to new levels of prosperity since it is rapidly becoming more efficient and cheaper. It is particularly suitable for developing nations. It is a driver for reducing poverty, social progress, equity, resilience, and economic growth. Producing renewable energy locally can benefit rural and remote areas. Hydropower is the largest source of renewable electricity while solar and wind energy are growing rapidly.

6.   *Global Approach:* To be impactful requires a global approach, engaging all levels of society – from communities, regions, and governments to numerous other stakeholders across the public and private sectors. The International Renewable Energy Agency (IRENA) is an intergovernmental organization that supports countries in their transition to a sustainable energy future and serves as the principal platform for international co-operation on renewable energy. IRENA promotes the widespread adoption and sustainable use of all forms of renewable energy, including bioenergy, geothermal, hydropower, ocean, solar, and wind energy, in the pursuit of sustainable development, energy access, energy security, economic growth, and prosperity. Figure 9.8 shows the inaugural session of the International Renewable Energy Agency (IRENA) Assembly that was held in April 2011 in Abu Dhabi [28].

Figure 9.8 The inaugural session of the IRENA Assembly [28].

7.   *Less Pollution:* Switching from coal to natural gas has advantages in terms of sustainability. It reduces emissions in the short term and thus contributes to climate change mitigation. Natural gas combustion also produces less air pollution than coal.

8.   *Future We Want:* Sustainable energy for all is an idea whose time has come. Working in partnership, governments, parliamentarians, private sector companies, industries, and civil society are making diverse contributions inspired by a unity of purpose. Sustainable Energy for All is about driving actions and mobilizing commitments to positively transform the world's energy systems. It seeks to achieve, by 2030, universal access to electricity and safe household fuels. Together, we can power a sustainable future free of poverty.

9.8 CHALLENGES

The most significant challenges to the widespread implementation of sustainable energy are seen to be mainly social and political, not mainly technological or economic. The key barriers to adoption of sustainable energy include climate change denial, the fossil fuels lobby, political inaction, higher generation cost, higher market price, unsustainable energy consumption, outdated energy infrastructure, and expanding access to affordable, reliable, and adequate energy supplies. Renewable energy from sources such as wind power and solar power is sometimes criticized for being variable and not available 24/7. Hydroelectric power generators can disrupt river ecosystems both upstream and downstream from the dam. The persistent critical challenge is to ensure an improved quality of life and economic growth, while reducing the environmental footprint of the energy sector. Other challenges of sustainable energy include the following [26,29,30].

1.   *Cost:* Sustainable energy technology has sometimes been regarded as expensive by critics, and affordable only in the affluent developed world. But sustainable energy can be suitable for developing countries as well. It can contribute to poverty reduction by providing the energy needed for creating businesses and jobs. Sustainable energy will require affordability and cost effectiveness in a competitive marketplace.

2.   *Accessibility:* Nearly one out of five persons on the planet still lacks access to energy or electricity. These people still rely on wood, coal, charcoal or animal waste for cooking and heating. This is a major barrier to eradicating poverty and building shared prosperity. There is rural-urban divide in electricity access, underscoring the fact that rural electrification rates in many nations remain low. Lack of access to energy supplies and transformation systems is a constraint to human and economic development.

3.   *Availability of Finance:* Economic constrain is a challenge, as substantial investment is needed to implement sustainable energy. Investment in sustainable energy depends on the availability of finance. Developed economies dominated the financing of sustainable energy. In developing economies, investing in sustainable energy technology is difficult because of the high cost of financing and also because obtaining financing at affordable rates is a major challenge.

4.   *Policy Making:* Addressing the issue of sustainable energy requires the engagement of the broad group of stakeholders. Energy professionals and leaders need to understand the use sustainable energy in legislation and organizational decision-making. Policies can be effective at driving behavior. For example, a policymaker who drafts a green bill only using the term "renewable energy" may subvert the effect of their own legislation by failing to account for the potential environmental impact of energy sources like biofuels.

5. *Nuclear Power:* Advances in deploying renewables have been mostly offset by declining shares of nuclear power. The sustainability of nuclear power which is a low-carbon source is highly debated. There is controversy over whether nuclear power is sustainable, in part due to concerns around nuclear waste, nuclear weapon proliferation, and accidents. Reducing the time and the cost of building new nuclear plants have been goals for decades but costs remain high and timescales long. Many countries are attempting to develop nuclear fusion reactors, which would generate small amounts of waste and no risk of explosions.

6. *Behavioral Change:* For a society to replace one form of energy with another, multiple technologies and behaviors in the energy system must change. Behavioral changes such as making urban trips by cycling, walking or public transport rather than by car, are another way to conserve energy. Policies, laws, business mechanisms, and regulations can drive behavior.

7. *Political Will:* Political will is necessary to accomplish the transition from brown to green energy. There is an incentive to use 100%renewable energy to help confront issues related to climate change, energy security, and the escalation of energy costs. Each country should have sustainable energy as an important component of their energy planning. Government policies are important in ensuring that the energy sector produces sustainable energy. Policy instruments such as taxes, regulations, and subsidies can stimulate the adoption of green energy technologies. Hindrances may also be due to corporate lobbying, political pressure, and inherent dependence on fossil fuels.

8. *Energy Storage:* This helps overcome barriers to intermittent renewable energy and is an important aspect of a sustainable energy system. Batteries typically store electricity for short periods. Battery storage helps protect the end user from utility rate changes and allows them to maximize the time of day when batteries are charged and discharge, when the utility rates are greatest. Low energy density of batteries makes them impractical for the very large energy storage.

9. *Power to Rural Areas:* One of the challenges in providing universal access to electricity is distributing power to rural areas. It is difficult to provide sustainable energy to areas less likely to

produce it. Off-grid and mini-grid systems based on renewable energy that generate and store enough electricity for rural communities are important solutions.

Figure 9.9 shows some of these challenges.

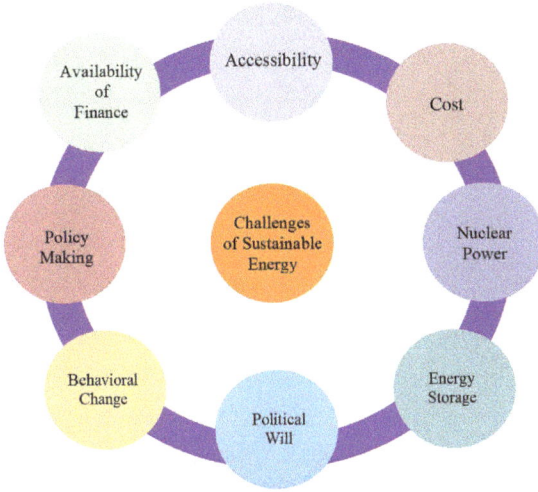

Figure 9.5 A geothermal power plant [12].

9.9 CONCLUSION

Energy plays a vital role in the economic growth, progress, development, and security of any nation. It is fundamental for socioeconomic development and poverty eradication. It is both an enabler and a challenge for sustainable development.

Globalization has led the modern society towards green or sustainable sources of energy, which are clean sources of energy with a lower environmental impact compared to traditional conventional energy source. Sustainable energy has attracted much attention across the globe due to the fact that it is non-polluting and more environmental-friendly.

Creating a sustainable energy future is one of the world's greatest challenge. Only through sustainable energy is our energy consumption today does not compromise the needs of future generations. For environmental, energy security, and economic reasons, sustainable energy is the future. It has generated millions of jobs around the world.

Millions of sustainable energy jobs will be available for qualified workers over the coming decade. Training and education are essential in preparing workers to take advantage of these opportunities. More education about sustainable energy is necessary for the general public, students, and engineers to be aware of the new field. More information about sustainable energy can be found in the books in [31-50] and in the journals devoted to sustainable energy:

- *Energy*
- *Applied Energy*
- *Energy Journal*
- *Journal of Sustainable Energy Engineering*
- *Journal of Sustainable Energy Revolution*
- *Journal of Renewable Energy and Sustainable Development*
- *Renewable and Sustainable Energy Reviews*
- *International Journal of Sustainable Energy*
- *International Journal of Green Energy*
- *IEEE Transactions on Sustainable Energy*

REFERENCE

[1]   M. N. O. Sadiku, S. R. Nelatury, and S.M. Musa, "Green energy: A primer," Journal of Scientific and Engineering Research, vol. 5, no. 7, 2018, pp. 336-339.

[2]   A. S. Sambo, "The way forward for sustainable energy supply in Nigeria," Unknown Source.

[3]   S. A. R. Khan and D. Qianli, "Does national scale economic and environmental indicators spur logistics performance? Evidence from UK," Environmental Science and Pollution Research, vol. 24, no. 34, December 2017, pp. 26692–26705.

[4]   S. Brown, "A case for green energy manufacturing," New Solutions, vol. 19, no. 2, 2009, pp. 135-137.

[5]   D. Lidgate, " Green energy?" Engineering Science and Education Journal, October 1992, pp. 221-227.

[6]   C. Bhowmik, S. Bhowmik, and A. Ray, "Social acceptance of green energy determinants using principal component analysis," Energy, vol. 160, 2018, pp. 1030-1046.

[7]   M. Jefferson, "Energy policies for sustainable development,"

https://www.undp.org/sites/g/files/zskgke326/files/publications/chapter12.pdf

[8]   P. A. Adekunte, M. N. O. Sadiku, and J. O. Sadiku, "Sustainable energy," submitted for publication.

[9]   "What is the difference between renewable and sustainable energy?

https://www.prysmiangroup.com/en/insight/innovation/what-is-the-difference-between-renewable-and-sustainable-energy

[10]   "Types of green,"

https://www.igsenergy.com/your-energy-choices/green-energy/types-of-green/

[11]   "7 types of renewable energy to support commercial

sustainability,"

http://businessfeed.sunpower.com/lists/7-types-of-renewable-commercial-energy

[12] R. Ramirez, "5 Alternative energy sources to speed our transition away from fossil fuels,"

https://krdo.com/news/national-world/cnn-national/2021/10/07/5-alternative-energy-sources-to-speed-our-transition-away-from-fossil-fuels/

[13]" What is a wind turbine and how it works,"

https://engineeringdiscoveries.com/what-is-a-wind-turbine-and-how-it-works/

[14] "Renewable energy vs sustainable energy: What's the difference?" July 2021,

https://energy.sais.jhu.edu/articles/renewable-energy-vs-sustainable-energy/

[15]   T. Dillahunt et al., "It's not all about 'green:' Energy use in low-income communities," Proceedings of the 11th international conference on Ubiquitous computing, Orlando, Florida, September -October, 2009, pp. 255-264.

[16]   D. Nag et al., "Green energy powered smart healthy home," Proceedings of the 8th Annual Industrial Automation and Electromechanical Engineering Conference,

August 2017, pp. 47-51.

[17] "Evolution solar,"

http://kingaroy.evolutionsolar.com.au/solar-power/solar-power-explained-evolution-solar-kingaroy/

[18] "9 ways businesses can benefit from renewable energy,"

https://www.conserve-energy-future.com/9-ways-businesses-can-benefit-renewable-energy.php

[19] R. Tripathi, S. Vignesh, and V. Tamarapalli, "Optimizing green energy, cost, and availability in distributed data centers," IEEE

Communications Letters, vol. 21, no. 3, March 2017, pp. 500-503.

[20]   F. Kong and X. Li, "A survey on green-energy-aware power management for datacenters," ACM Computing Surveys, vol. 47, no. 2, November 2014.

[21]   "Benefits of using edge data centers," March 2016, https://softwarefocus.net/bigdata/benefits-of-using-edge-data-centers.html

[22]   T. Han and N. Ansari, "Powering mobile networks with green energy," IEEE Wireless Communications, February 2014, pp. 90-96.

[23]   A. Jahid, A. B. Shams, and F. Hossain , "Green energy driven cellular networks with JT CoMP technique," Physical Communication, vol. 28, 2018, pp. 58–68.

[24]   "Renewable energy," Wikipedia, the free encyclopedia https://en.wikipedia.org/wiki/Renewable_energy

[25]   "Benefits of renewable energy use," https://www.ucsusa.org/clean-energy/renewable-energy/public-benefits-of-renewable-power#.WxBWYk0o7nMContents

[26]   "Sustainable energy," Wikipedia, the free encyclopedia, https://en.wikipedia.org/wiki/Sustainable_energy

[27]   "Sustainable Energy for All - Global tracking framework," November 26, 2015, https://www.undp.org/publications/sustainable-energy-all-global-tracking-framework

[28] "The global governance of sustainable energy: Access and sustainable transitions," https://www.iisd.org/articles/global-governance-sustainable-energy

[29] D. Timmons, J. M. Harris, and B. Roach, The Economics of Renewable Energy.

Medford, MA: Global Development and Environment Institute, 2014.

[30]   M. Woerter et al., "The adoption of green energy technologies:

The role of policies in Austria, Germany, and Switzerland," International Journal of Green Energy, vol. 14, no. 14, 2017, pp. 1192-1208.

[31]   X. Li (ed.), Green Energy: Basic Concepts and Fundamentals. Springer, 2011.

[32]   D. Elliott (ed.), Sustainable Energy: Opportunities and Limitations. Springer 2007.

[33]   E. Jeffs, Greener Energy Systems: Energy Production Technologies with Minimum Environmental Impact. Boca Raton, FL: CRC Press, 201

[34]   E. Jeffs, Green Energy: Sustainable Electricity Supply with Low Environmental Impact. Boca Raton, FL: CRC Press, 2017.

[35]   U. Aswathanarayana, T. Harikrishnan, T. S. Kadher-Mohien, Green Energy: Technology, Economics and Policy. Boca Raton, FL: CRC Press, 2010.

[36]   J. Byrne, and Y. D. Wang, Green Energy Economies: The Search for Clean and Renewable Energy. Boca Raton, FL: CRC Press, 2014.

[37]   Y. Demirel, Energy: Production, Conversion, Storage, Conservation, and Coupling. Springer, 2nd ed., 2016.

[38]   R. T. D. Prabhakaran, S. A. Kale, and K. Prabakar (eds.), Renewable Energy and Sustainable Development. Nova Science Publishers, 2015.

[39]   R. A. Dunpal, Sustainable Energy. Cengage, 2nd edition, 2018.

[40]   J. A. Kilner et al. (eds.), Functional Materials for Sustainable Energy Applications. Elsevier, 2012.

[41]   E. Boeker and R. V. Grondelle. Environmental Physics: Sustainable Energy and Climate Change. John Wiley & Sons, 2011.

[42]   P. Kruger, Alternative Energy Resources: The Quest for Sustainable Energy. Hoboken: Wiley, 2006.

[43]   C. Mitchell, The Political Economy of Sustainable Energy.

Basingstoke: Palgrave Macmillan, 2008.

[44] V. Dusastre (ed.), Materials for Sustainable Energy: A Collection of Peer-Reviewed Research and Review Articles From Nature Publishing Group. World Scientific, 2010.

[45] H. O. Paksoy (ed.), Thermal Energy Storage for Sustainable Energy Consumption: Fundamentals, Case Studies and Design. Vol. 234. Springer Science & Business Media, 2007

[46] J. W. Tester et al., Sustainable Energy: Choosing Among Options. MIT press, 2012.

[47] I. Dincer and C. Zamfirescu, Sustainable Energy Systems and Applications. Springer Science & Business Media, 2011.

[47] F. Kreith and S. Krumdieck, Principles of Sustainable Energy Systems. Boca Raton, FL: CRC Press, 2013.

[48] E. S. Cassedy, Prospects for Sustainable Energy: A Critical Assessment. Cambridge University Press, 2000.

[49] M. Diesendorf, Greenhouse Solutions with Sustainable Energy. Sydney, Australia:: University of New South Wales Press, 2007.

[50] D. J. C. MacKay, Sustainable Energy-without the Hot Air. Bloomsbury Publishing, 2016.

INDEX

www.ingramcontent.com/pod-product-compliance
Lightning Source LLC
Chambersburg PA
CBHW041930260326
41914CB00009B/1249